"where do we start, on the threshold, before a door.
Here it is - simplified so we can see its complexities. . .
doors are very potent symbols."

By same author

Tankhem: Seth & Egyptian Magick

The Bull of Ombos (Seth & Egyptian Magick II)

Supernatural Assault in Ancient Egypt

The Wheel of the Year in Ancient Egypt

(with Soror Nephthys) *The Desert Fox Oracle*

Phi-Neter:

The power of the Egyptian Gods

Heka (Magick)
& Akhw (Spells)

Published by
Mandrake of Oxford
PO Box 250
OXFORD
OX1 1AP (UK)

"According to ... a fable which Diodorus and Ovid tell about Typhon, he is seen as the personification of inquisitiveness and impious curiosity, the very character that is so dangerous for the pseudo-gods. The fable tells how the gods fled to Egypt before Typhon and hid there in the shape of animals. Typhon is the Greek equivalent of the Egyptian God Seth, who is actually represented in the Egyptian texts as threatening the gods with the sacrilegious discovery of their secrets. According to the Egyptians, the secret of the gods is not . . . their mortal past, but something not totally unrelated to the idea of mortality. The paradigmatic secret, in Egypt, is the corpse of Osiris, which must by all means be protected against the assaults of Seth. . ."

Jan Assmann *Moses The Egyptian* :
the memory of Egypt in western monotheism, Harvard : 112

Contents

DEDICATED TO THE SMAUT EN SET

Introduction

THE EGYPTIAN MAGICAL-RELIGION

"Ancient Egypt is an intellectual and spiritual world that
is linked to our own by numerous strands of tradition."
Jan Assmann, *The Mind of Egypt*

Phi-Neter, means 'Power of the Gods'. In hieroglyphs this is represented
by the hind-quarters of a leopard, the driving force of this powerful
predator.

This is followed by the sign usually thought to be a flag, although it
might also be some kind of wrapped fetish or *packette* of a kind commonly
found in Voodoo or the African based religions of the Americas. So this
book comprises an exploration of magick (*heka*), the casting of spells
(*akhw*) and various other means to set in motion the divine powers of
the ancient Egyptian Gods.

The Latin term *magick* is useful but also loaded with Roman bias that
has haunted any discussion of its techniques for the last 2000 years.
The Egyptian magician wields a power that was ultimately created by
the Gods for the use of anyone who wishes to do their work. It's the

same underlying power whether manipulated by Gods, priests, aristocrats, the common people or even the criminal. Same power, different ends.[1]

I first learnt of this mythos via the Hermetic Order of the Golden Dawn, probably the most famous occult sodality of modern times. Founded in 1888 it had largely ceased activities by the early 1920s. Even so there are a number of contemporary groups who claim to be successors to its mantle and there is hardly any modern initiate who has not either heard of or used some of its techniques and ideas.

It was for this reason that in 1981 a small group of novice initiates in Oxford formed their own Golden Dawn Occult Society as homage to the late 19th century original. My fellow initiates were of the opinion that one of many valid successors to the Golden Dawn was the celebrated magus Aleister Crowley. No doubt more traditional Golden Dawn aficionados would turn a jaundiced eye on such a suggestion; especially given the fact that many blame Aleister Crowley for the premature death of the esteemed order. Controversially, Crowley published the principal rituals of the Hermetic Order of the Golden Dawn in his journal *The Equinox*. Later, Israel Regardie, one of Crowley's most gifted students, completed the process with the publication of a *Complete Golden Dawn System of Magick*, the source of much subsequent work with these ideas. Perhaps one can see that, as pretentious as the Oxford initiates might appear, there was some method in their madness.

Over the years these ideas have been revised and supplemented in the light of my own journey of more than two decades into the magick of

---

1.   Robert Ritner (1993) *The Mechanics of Ancient Egyptian Magical Practice*, Chicago University Press

ancient Egypt. I am not claiming any special insider knowledge or initiation. Neither am I any longer interested in reviving the old sodality in any organizational sense. I am an outsider. Even so it pleases me to return to the original optimism I had when first starting out in magick. I hope it will cast an interesting light on the inspiration of those eminent Victorian adepts who did so much to set the current occult revival in motion.

I have come to believe that the real 'Golden Dawn' is an experience rather than an organization. Apart from poetic insights, this book is in the main a short and simple excursion into the ancient Egyptian magical religion. My aim is to offer a workable summary of freeform Egyptian magick supplementing material already revealed and/or presented in earlier works from which I will extract vital bits of information as needed.

You may wonder why I use the term 'freeform'. Contemporary guides to Egyptian magick imply that it is anything but *freeform*. Isn't Egyptian magick very formal and theatrical? Pretty much all contemporary books present it as so. Consider this - if an ancient Egyptian were to teleport to contemporary London during the opening ceremony for the 2012 Olympics - would they be witness to a neo-pagan ceremony? Well in part maybe, especially Patrick Hetherington's *Olympic flame*. Viewing this spectacle changed my mind and showed me how such mass gatherings can be magick. Ancient Egypt had similar mass events but in my view the core of the tradition transpired on a much more personal and human scale. Monumental public spectacles of ancient Egypt were nourished by the personal and the private. So try to put aside what you know and approach the surviving records of ancient Egyptian magick with a fresh mind.

THE FALSE DOOR

I have found the image of the Egyptian 'false door' an evocative entry point into the tradition. The image is based upon ancient examples. I have simplified it in order to bring out its complexity, its geometrical and "liminal" elements..

(The manner in which I reduced it to its "seed" meaning owes much to the visual techniques of the Hermetic Order of the Golden Dawn. The Order made creative use of "flashing colours", colours such as red and green. It also popularized heavily contrasted "sigils" in matt black and white as a means of evoking magical consciousness in the viewer. The source of these techniques undoubtedly lies in the visual culture of ancient Egypt.

To experience a flashing colour, get some coloured construction paper. Cut out a blue circle four inches in diameter and place it on a red square of similar dimensions. Lay them out on a table top and view by candle light. The image will oscillate and move around. Close your eyes and look at the after-image!

A door is a very potent symbol. Knowledge of the whole of the Egyptian magical religion is latent in this ancient image of a door. Experts on the Egyptian "false" or *Ka* door[2] usually discuss it in conjunction with an object known as a stele - a stone or wooden slab of varying size, inscribed with text and pictures and most commonly used at the threshold of a tomb, as a votive offering in a holy place or as part of a personal shrine in the home. The stele and the false door have much in common.

---

2. *Šeb3 Kr, šh-Kᶜ, šh Neter*

The door is "false" only in the sense that it bars the way for the physical body but allows the spirits of the living and the dead to pass through. It is the interface between our world and the Otherworld. I recommend calling this image to mind in meditation or ritual as a portal to an ancient Egypt which still exists in the imaginal realm. I will return to the motif of the false door in more detail below.

It would be useful at this point to call to mind the idea of the astral temple within the Western mystery tradition. There are several good books on the topic including *Tankhem* (Morgan 2005). One important refinement is that one should base one's astral temple on an actual building, even if only the archaeological plans.

The other is to "sleep" in the temple. This is facilitated by having a representation of the "false door" in your bedroom, positioned such that it is the last thing you see before sleep. Sleep as absolutely the most important arena of Egyptian magick.

NOT TEMPLE

Thinking about magical doors inevitably brings to mind the issue of location for Egyptian magick. A temple is the place but less obvious but in my opinion of equal importance is the space *outside* the temple.

By "not the temple" I mean everything that happens in magick that is outside of the formal temple space. This could literally be just outside the temple walls, perhaps outside the back wall of the holy of holies. I kid you not, archaeological research has revealed that the places immediately behind the temple holy of holies was a hotspot of ritual activity. Take for example the Osireion at Abydos, one of the most important ritual sites in Upper Egypt. One makes one's approach to this shrine via a path that lies *outside* of the main temple *temenos* or sacred barrier.*

One of my scholarly mentors told me that Egyptian magick was so powerful it was only really safe when practiced in the temple. She viewed the temple as a complex piece of ritual mechanics. She has a point - most people can still sense the power in surviving Egyptian temples despite their ruinous condition.

Existentially we are outside the temple whether we like it or not, so we have to make the best of it. And as it happens, for most Egyptian the elaborate temple was a "black box" from which the folk (the *Rekhyt*) were largely excluded. Apart from the outer courtyards, the interiors of Egyptian temples were peopled by priests and their aristocratic patrons. There are of course important moments during which the two spaces come together.

There is an ebb and flow between these groups and spaces. I'd remind you that with some exceptions, there was no permanent priesthood in ancient Egypt. All those qualified to do so, male and female, might serve as priest at some time in their lives. I like this model of how the priesthood should be organized. To my mind it is so appropriate for our contemporary magical world. The shifts or "phyle" of priests worked one month in every ten according to a rota regulated by a lunar calendar.[3]

---

* **Temenos**: a sacred territory, circle or field, usually marked out by a boundary within which is the domain of deity or divinity. Commonly the temple sits within the temenos together with other buildings, for example *magazines* used to store materials used in the religious activity.

3. Barry Kemp (2006) *Ancient Egypt: Anatomy of a Civilization*, Routledge : 113

A long time ago I parted company on rather bad terms with one of my first mentors in Khemetic magick. He knew of my calling to the *Companions* of Seth and his final grudging advice was that I should investigate the temple of Sety I at Abydos. I did and over time began to view this as my *omphalos*, not exclusively for the ancient Egyptians but for much of the classical world of the time. Its physical fabric is nowadays much depleted; even so there is an *archaeological* memory from which we can still benefit.

In fact I learnt so much it became a central part of my vision of a Khemetic Golden Dawn. Most of those trained in Golden Dawn techniques work on the physical plane but also in the imaginal or astral world. One's first access to this "imaginarium" is facilitated by plans of an idealised temple. Often this is based on the legendary temple of King Solomon described in the *Bible, Book of Kings* 6 1-39; 7; & 8. For many this functions as an "astral" or imaginal temple, envisioned as being in the sphere of *Malkuth* on the Golden Dawn Tree of Life. But even this Solomonic temple has a hidden Egyptian componant: "The holy of holies . . . an enclosed, windowless cube of wood, with sides each measuring about 10 metres, appears to have been an adaptation of an Egyptian tradition about a chapel of the Gods."[5] This being so then it also makes a lot of sense to return to older, primal models such as the temple of Sety I at Abydos.

Like everyone else my first magical exercises involved the visualisation of the primal doorway of the astral temple. Back in the day I was guided

---

5.   Othmar Keel & , Christoph Uehlinger (1998) *Gods, Goddesses and images of God in Ancient Israel*, Edinburg : 167

to create a sacred space or *temenos* using a ritual called the Lesser Ritual of the Pentagram (LRP).

THE EGYPTIAN MAGICK OF ABRAMELIN

Since its publication in 1897, *The Book of Abramelin* has been much celebrated by occultists. Scattered throughout this book are instructions for a ritual which will reputably open the doors of the unconscious and bestow great magical knowledge and power. Even a cursory examination of this book reveals a debt to Egyptian temple practice. The book provided the working methods for the Hermetic Order of the Golden Dawn, who broke it all down into graduated steps by which the initiate could pass through the door of ignorance and ascend to gnosis. To this day these techniques underlie pretty much all occult ritualism.

Book III Chapter 7 provides the basic description - the candidate begins his or her rite by rising early just before dawn. This is precisely the moment at which the ritual day began in ancient Egypt. The ritual year began on the first morning of Passover or Easter, also an important day. After performing ablutions and wearing clean clothes, the priest entered a special prayer room or *Naos*. He opens the eastern window then kneels in front of his altar and prays to "mister" that he send a messenger (HGA or Holy Guardian Angel) to instruct him in the secrets of the universe. This rubrik offers no traditional or formal words for the prayer - the priest must speak from the heart in his or her own language. When done, the priest closes the eastern window and leaves the room, returning after sunset to repeat the whole procedure. In the version published by

6. *The Book of the Sacred Magic of Abramelin the Mage* translated by S.L. MacGregor Mathers (1897; reprinted by Dover Publications, 1975)

MacGregor Mathers the rite continues for six months followed by three days of revelation. In the more recent Georg Dehn version the whole practice takes 18 months. [6]

Living and sleeping space is in an antechamber outside, although occasional, especially in the climax of this work, one may need to sleep in the prayer room.

Using details in chapter seven and later chapter eleven it is clear how the layout of the prayer room closely resembles the standard Egyptian temple space. The holy of holies is a cubic room. There should be a strong sense of cardinality - north-south, east-west. Few houses lend themselves to such a precise orientation but there again neither did those of Egyptian temples, which often had to cope with a *nominal* or virtual north based on the flow of the river Nile. Basically there is an entrance in the south, a false door in the north (the place of midnight) and two windows opening to the east and west. In the centre is a monolithic altar, or one conveniently constructed of wood. If one does sleep in the prayer room it should be near the southernmost entrance door.

Here follows a ground plan:

---

7. *Abraham Von Worms, The Book of Abramelin : a new translation being a complete and modern translation from various extant manuscripts, including a previously unpublished fourth part.* Compiled and edited by Georg Dehn, translation by Steven Guth (IBIS 2006)

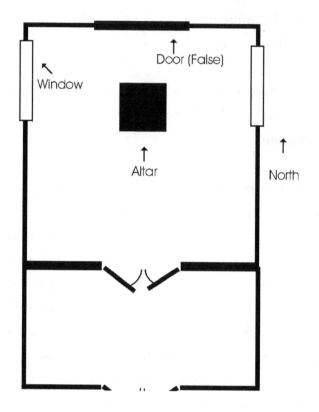

Temple floorplans often do end up echoing the inner structure of the mind and are for this reasons sometimes called "mind-maps". Even if you never undertake the "formal" Abramelin rite, just looking at the plan cannot fail to make you more aware of the primal wirings of your own mind. You could also consider it a precursor to something known in the East as *Feng Shui* - Chinese Geomancy. Not many people have the option to construct an ideal ritual space this way. Even so it may be possible to incorporate some small changes that will have a big impact on consciousness.

These geomantic ideas are common to Abramelin, ancient Egypt, the Orient, and not surprisingly Islam, from which some of it filtered back into Western magic. Look at this detail below which shows a typical floorplan of the "holy of holies" or barque shrine from the Temple of Sety I at Abydos. You should see the similarities.

Abramelin belongs to a class of books called *grimoires*. Most grimoires are pretty nonsensical – or put it another way perhaps we are meant to be entertained. Back in the 15th century and maybe always – people enjoyed a mysterious or scary story. Seen this way, the grimoire is the precursor to the novel. Abramelin certainly begins with an adventure story:

Take this example of raising the dead:

> "All the high-ranking spirits take part in this work. All it
> takes is to do the following: as soon as the person dies,
> lay the word square on him after the fourth part of the
> day. As soon as he moves, and begins to sit up, dress

him in new clothes. Inside the clothes sew a word square like was placed on his body. Whenever new clothes are worn, the word square needs to be placed inside.

It is not possible to extend the time past seven years. At exactly the point that the spirit again becomes one with the body the person will suddenly collapse. I myself saw an example of this when a dead duke - whose name I do not want to mention - who reanimated and was preserved on earth for seven years. Then, the young duke - his son - reached the correct age and was able to retain possession of the kingdom, which without this method would have fallen under the authority of foreign lands." [8]

Although part entertainment this need not preclude them containing genuine truths, of being "A fantasy but also true". In amongst all the fantastic claims of magic power are philosophical nuggets such as "He who abandons his natural law or embraces another religion opposed to his own, can never arrive at the summit of the sacred science." [9]

Abramelin is a book of many parts. It begins with a magical journey from medieval Europe to ancient Egypt. Parallel to this it urges us to undertake an inner journey invoking one's "Guardian Angel". Together you will be able to raise and control the denizens of the demonic realm;

---

8.   Abramelin 2006 : 137. Mathers in his 1897 : 217 names the subject as Duke of Saxonia, perhaps Erik IV, who reunited the Saxe-Lauenburg lineage (1401–1876). In Mathers' version Abraham is said to have actually performed the miracle.

9.   Abramelin Book I 46

the demon kings and their vassals and to do this in complete confidence and safety.

Abraham of Wurms was, according to Georg Dehn, a real 15th century magus. He studied with various teachers, mainly Kabbalists. He bequeathed his knowledge of the mysteries of Kabbalah to his oldest son; those of magick to his youngest (Lamech). To his daughters he left a handsome blob of money.

Abramelin was the name of Abraham's Egyptian teacher. They met after Abraham's long pilgrimage across Europe to Constantinople and there on to Palestine, Arabia then to a place called Arachi or Araki near the Nile.

Al Araki is a small Upper Egyptian town near Qina just off a long route that in ancient times connected the western desert to the Red Sea. His route is therefore feasible. In his account he says he walked 3½ days from there into the desert. Is that symbolic? There is also a track near Al Araki across the mountains to Luxor via Thoth Hill. Here, deep in the mountains, in a very ancient spot on the northern face of "pyramid mountain" is the 11th dynasty tomb of Mentuhotep III.

Although the pharaonic remains on Thoth Hill are long abandoned, even in antiquity, they were reused as religious sanctuaries, and this was in part because they retained an odour of sanctity. Hence in the 4-5th century, Saint Paul the Hermit, built his small hermitage in the tomb. The tomb itself was built near an earlier pharaonic temple, which was itself built on even older temple ruins which has been aligned to the star Sirius. Which all goes to show how a story can have interesting connections.

In Egypt, even today, tombs can be places of contact with the local Genii, Djinn or Genius. There is even a special class of Djinn connected with ancient tombs - *Shaytan Faraon* (Pharaonic Shaytan)? [10]

It was perhaps in such a place that Abraham of Wurms met his teacher Abramelin. He may well have been an Islamic specialist in magick, perhaps a Sufi or Sheikh. When the training was finished, Abramelin allowed his student to make copies of the magical books in his possession, the rest is publishing history.

The Book of Abramelin view the spirits (or Djinn) as part of a hierarchy. At the pinacle is the Sun-God and below that are four Kings:
Lucifer, Satan, Leviathan and Belial.
Next in line are eight Dukes:
Astoroth, Magot, Asmodee & Belzebub
Oriens, Paimon, Ariton, Ahaimon.
These princes rule over approximately 360 lesser spirits.

Georg Dehn draws our attention to the grouping created by Franz Bardon (1909-1958) in his book *The Practice of Magical Invocation*.[11] Following Bardon's lead, we might better use the Egyptian schema of decans or ten day periods. The entire Egyptian year consisted of 36 ten day weeks.

---

10. Hans Alexander Winkler (2009) *Ghost Riders of Upper Egypt*; Kees van der Spek (2010) *The Modern Neighbors of Tutankhamun, History, Life, and Work in the Villages of the Theban West Bank*.

11. Dehn (2006 : 257) The total number of spirits varies from one manuscript to another - Peter Hammer's published in Cologne in 1725 numbers them as 360. Bardon divided these 360 spirits into 30 groups of 12.

This older Egyptian classification is also the key to their "daemons" and is undoubtedly the origin of the medieval list.

If we omit the names of the Dukes, a new list emerges. It is quite long and its utility might not be obvious at this stage. But for the record:

ABRAMELIN DAEMONS & EGYPTIAN DECANS

1. Morech, Serep, Proxone, Nablum, Kosem,
   Peresh, Thirana, Aluph, Neschamah, Milon,

2. Frasis, Haja, Malacha, Molabeda, Yparcha,
   Nudatoni, Methaera, Bruahi, Apollyon, Schaluah,

3. Myrmo, Melamo, Pother, Schad, Echdulon,
   Manmes, Obedomah, Iachil, Ivar, Moschel,

4. Peekah, Hasperim, Kathim, Porphora, Badet,
   Kohen, Lurchi, Falfuna, Padidi, Helali,

5. Mahra, Rascheä, Nogah, Adae, Erimites,
   Trapi, Naga, Echami, Aspadit, Nasi,

6. Peralit, Emfalion, Paruch, Girmil, Tolet,
   Helmis, Asinel, Ionion, Asturel, Flabiscon,

7. Nascela, Conioli, Isnirki, Pliroki, Aslotama,
   Zagriona, Parmasa, Sarasi, Geriola, Afonono,

8. Liriell, Alagill, Opollogon, Carubot, Morilon, Losimon, Kagaros, Ygilon, Gesegos, Ugefor,

9. Asoreg, Paruchu, Siges, Atherom, Ramara, Jajaregi, Golema, Kiliki, Romasara, Alpaso,

10. Soteri, Amillee, Ramage, Pormatho, Metosee, Porascho, Anamil, Orienell, Timiran, Oramos,

11. Anemalon, Kirek, Batamabub, Ranar, Namalon, Ampholion, Abusis, Egention, Tabori, Concario,

12. Golemi, Tarato, Tabbata, Buriuh, Omana, Caraschi, Dimurga, Kogid, Panfodra, Siria

13. Igigi, Dosom, Darachin, Horomor, Ahahbon, Yraganon, Lagiros, Eralier, Golog, Cemiel,

14. Hagus, Vollman, Bialode, Galago, Bagoloni, Tmako, Akanejohano, Argaro, Afrei, Sagara,

15. Ugali, Erimihala, Hatuny, Hagomi, Opilon, Paguldez, Paschy, Nimalon, Horog, Algebol,

16. Rigolon, Trasorim, Elason, Trisacha, Gagolchon, Klorecha, Irachro, Pafessa, Amami, Camalo,

17. Taxae, Karase, Riqita, Schulego, Giria, Afimo, Bafa, Baroa, Golog, Iromoni,

18. Pigios, Nimtrix, Herich, Akirgi, Tapum,
    Hipolopos, Hosun, Garses, Ugirpon, Gomognu,

19. Argilo, Tardoe, Cepacha, Kalote, Ychniag,
    Basanola, Nachero, Natolisa, Mesah, Mesadu,

20. Capipa, Fermetu, Barnel, Ubarim, Urgivoh,
    Ysquiron, Odac, Rotor, Arator, Butharusch,

21. Harkinson, Arabim, Koreh, Forsterton, Sernpolo,
    Magelucha, Amagestol, Sikesti, Mechebbera, Tigrapho,

22. Malata, Tagora, Petuna, Amia, Somi,
    Lotogi, Hyris, Chadail, Debam, Abagrion,

23. Paschan, Cobel, Arioth, Panari, Caboneton,
    Kamual, Erytar, Nearah, Hahadu, Charagi,

24. Kolani, Kibigili, Corocana, Hipogo, Agikus,
    Nagar, Echagi, Parachmo, Kosirma, Dagio,

25. Oromonas, Hagos, Mimosah, Arakuson, Rimog,
    Iserag, Cheikaseph, Kofan, Batirunos, Cochaly,

26. Ienuri, Nephasser, Bekaro, Hyla, Eneki,
    Maggio, Abbetira, Breffeo, Ornion, Schaluach,

27. Hillaro, Ybario, Altono, Armefia, Belifares,
    Camalo, Corilon, Dirilisin, Eralicarison, Elipinon,

28. Gariniranus, Sipillipis, Ergomion, Lotifar, Chimirgu,
    Kaerlesa, Nadele, Baalto, Ygarimi, Akahimo,

29. Golopa, Naniroa, Istaroth, Tedea, Ikon,
    Kama, Arisaka, Bileka, Yromus, Camarion,

30. Jamaih, Aragor, Igakis, Olaski, Haiamon,
    Semechle, Alosom, Segosel, Boreb, Ugolog,

31. Hadcu, Amalomi, Bilifo, Granona, Pagalusta,
    Hyrmiua, Canali, Radina, Gezero, Sarsiee,

32. Soesman, Tmiti, Balachman, Gagison, Mafalach,
    Zagol, Ichdison, Sumuram, Aglasis, Hachamel,

33. Agasoly, Kiliosa, Ebaron, Zalones, Jugula,
    Carahami, Kaflesi, Mennolika. Takarosa, Astolitu,

34. Merki, Anadi, Ekore, Rosora, Negani,
    Cigila, Secabmi, Calamos, Sibolas, Forfasan,

35. Andrachor, Notiser, Filakon, Horasul, Saris,
    Ekorim, Nelion, Ylemis, Calacha, Sapasani,

36. Seneol, Charonthona, Carona, Regerio, Megalogi,
    Irmana, Elami, Ramgisa, Sirigilis, Boria.

With the list rearranged this way we can perhaps make more sense of
the frequent references to the number 72 in the text.

Eg: "Abramelin asked if I had any money. I answered 'yes'. He asked me for 10 gold guilders which he - as an obligation to Adonai - was required to distribute to 72 people."[12]

72 is one of those special magical numbers that occurs again and again in magical contexts. It is for example an important number in ancient Egyptian astro-lore, being the average number of days in the yearly cycle a star is absent from the night sky. It is thus also the ideal number of days required to prepare a mummy to rise again. 5 x 72 = 360.

After the long performance of the ritual, either for six or more properly 12 plus six months is a religious experience in part ecstatic and part intellectual. The results are tabulated in the book's final section which deals with the *Magick Squares*.

MAGICK SQUARES

Magick Squares are very much part of the mechanics of late Egyptian magick. Given the importance of puns and word play in their construction, it seems likely they are an Egyptian innovations with a long history.

In our time one of the most well-known is the SATOR-AREPO square which is early Coptic Christian magick based on older Pagan techniques. Writing in the *Classical Review* the eminent Egyptologist Gwynn-Griffiths

---

12. Dehn (2006 : 16)

identifies one of the words as an Egyptian personal name AREPO, translating the entire square as:

"The farmer Arepo pushes his plough" [13]

SATOR,

AREPO

TENET

OPERA

ROTAS

In addition there is a second, secret message or *spell* hidden in the square, one that was only discovered in the early 20th century. If one regroups all the letters one finds the embedded *acrostic* (crossword):

Paternoster ("our father") Alpha and Omega

Acrostics, Palindromes and other word games are all part of an old "daemonic" and hidden language used by spirits to communicate with us and we with them. The oldest examples are Egyptian circa 1400BCE.[13]

---

13. Gwynn-Griffiths 1971 *The Classical Review* vol 21.i . Arepo is an Egyptian name (Hor-Hep). Other examples cited by Zandee are from time of Ramses II. See J Zandee (1966) *An Egyptian Crossword Puzzle*, Leiden.

Anthony Peake in his book *The Daemon* has an interesting modern psychological way of looking at *daemons*. Peake starts from the premise that we each have not one but two personalities. The ancient would have called these the "Daemon" and the "Eidolon".[14]

Several books have pointed to experiences we all have at key points in our lives where this dual personality seems to be at work. For example "The Old Hag" or "Night Shadow".

> Evil Sleep - You're in your bed, it's dark, you hear footsteps coming up the stairs and into your room. There's someone there - a presence. They lie on you or beside you, perhaps even gripping you tightly, crushing you into the bed. You can't move. There may be a sound, a grunt or a strange smell. Time passes, you are paralysed with fear. Eventually the entity changes, perhaps expanding or contracting, moving away from you, sinking to the floor. With a great effort of will you manage to move the tip of your finger, then the hand until movement returns to your whole body and the experience ends. You have been visited by the old 'hag'.

Magick explicitly aims to bridge the gap between both personalities, although the terminology "angel" or "daemon" is more common. The angel is perhaps the hidden, more powerful side of one's personality; otherwise angels and daemons are really very similar.

---

14. Anthony Peake (2010), *The Daemon: A Guide to Your Extraordinary Secret Self*, Arcturus.
15. David J Hufford, (1982) *The Terror that Comes in the Night: An experience centred study of supernatural assault traditions*

Occult lore stipulates that from the moment of your birth you are accompanied by a spiritual double. In modern speak: the brain has a dual-core processor. The organism is divided. Most people are unaware of this or if they are it is only through dreams or trance. The other personality, the "daemon", cannot speak directly but uses indirect methods to communicate in times of distress. Thus one must use some "occult" techniques to help things along.

The Book of Abramelin contains recipes for a unique perfume and incense for use in its experiments. Smell is the most primal of all the senses. One could perhaps look at several other occult techniques that in effect mediate this gap between the *labial* conscious self and the silent, inner daemon.

The use of a medium is another such method. Older texts suggest the use of a medium, often a "child". The first mediums were named after the Egyptian God Anubis, and because of a confusion of names, the idea arose that it had to be a child.[16] Even in 1930s Egypt, local children were used as mediums to talk to the spirits and search for buried treasure.

One's daemon may turn out to be of the opposite gender! In more class conscious ancient times, the higher one's social standing then the higher that of your "daemon". When the aristocrat "asks a friend" it might turn out to be a God.

When you die you are reunited with one's daemon, hence the Egyptians sometimes referred to death as "going to one's Ka". The magician is

---

16. *inpu*

continually trying to bridge the gap with the angel and hopes to complete the process before they die. For, so 'tis said, the "daemon has special powers which you do not. The daemon dwells in the *liminal* world of the spirits, therefore it may know the future.

CROWLEY & HIS DAEMON

Crowley was eventually put in touch with his *daemon* – Aiwass, an entity which some say was his own psyche. There is a famous photograph of Crowley posed with a magick book, a pentagram emblazoned on the front cover. What's in the book, nothing other than his complete collection of magick squares neatly drawn during his preparation for the Abramelin practice! [17]

The name of his angel lends itself to a bit of wordplay. Aiwass or "I Was" does indeed have a split personality, dictating a book that proposes

---

17   Frater Shiva (2012) *Inside Solar Lodge: Behind the Veil*, Desert Star Temple, p 773

entirely contradictory solutions to humanity's problems viz "The Law of the Jungle" versus "AL True Ism"? [18]

At the time of writing Aleister Crowley is still a force in modern magick. In so many ways he was the first modern magician.[19] 1904 was the pivotal year in Crowley's career. He was 29 years old and therefore well into what is popularly known as the "Saturn Return". [20]

Crowley had just got married although neither his or the bride's family were pleased with the match. He'd pretty much given up on the magick of his youth. The newlyweds were in Egypt – which coincidentally is for magicians, an important rite of passage. Every self-respecting magician is almost *required* to go there and make contact with the "Secret Chiefs".

The prequel to this journey was Crowley's experiments with the already mentioned *Book of Abramelin*. Crowley had been advised by his magical teacher George Cecil Jones to fully master its techniques. He therefore scoured Scotland for a suitable house and bought one called Boleskine overlooking Loch Ness. Some say his arrival re-awakened the famous resident monster!

---

18. Mogg Morgan, "The Heart of Thelema: Morality, Amorality, and Immorality in Aleister Crowley's Thelemic Cult" *Pomegranate: The International Journal of Pagan Studies*, Vol 13, No 2 (2011)

19. Lawrence Sutin (2000) *Do What Thou Wilt: A life of Aleister Crowley* NY

20. Saturn takes approximately 30 years to orbit the Sun and return to point in the sky it occupied near one's birth. Astrological lore contends that the end of one's third decade on the planet is influenced by saturnine thoughts etc.

His embarked on the crash course version of the rite, allocating just six lunar months for completion. In the 15th century, Abraham began his retreat at Easter (Jewish Passover) itself a very important ancient feast connected with demons and angels of death. These myths make use of doorways of one kind or another, the ancient Hebrews supposedly inscribing magick signs on their lintels, a signal for the angel of death to *passover* the house.

The ritual continues from equinox to equinox – starting the day after Passover or at the nearest new Moon, continuing until the full Moon after the autumn equinox. The practice therefore makes good use of a specific astro-symbolic segment of the year.

It terminated on the old feast of Tabernacles or "Booths". The modern interpretation tells us this was originally a reminder of the temporary dwellings used by the early Hebrews during their flight from Egypt. Other than the Biblical and Koranic accounts, the flight from Egypt is not corroborated by any other textual or archaeological evidence. It may be pure myth. However the feast of Tabernacles was also the first festival celebrated after the resumption of religious activity following the Babylonian captivity.

Another possible purpose of this feast was to celebrate a successful harvest. There is an equivalent Egyptian feast of Min in month II of Egyptian year, and this involved portable shrines or *booths*.

Six months of continuous practice proved too much for such a mercurial figure as Crowley. He was soon distracted – magical war had broken out within the Order of the Golden Dawn and he answered the call to arms. It all ended in farce but that's another story.

As for *The Book of Abramelin*, the magical moment had passed and there was no point in returning to Boleskine until the following Easter. So Crowley travelled to Mexico and as often happens did not return for several years. When he did he was again distracted by his future wife Rose Kelly. They headed off on the *grand tour* via the Suez Canal. Stopping in Cairo on April 8th, 9th & 10th 1904 at precisely the right moment to restart the rite - the rest, as they say, is history.

THE KHEMETIC VERSION OF THE LESSER RITUAL OF THE PENTAGRAM (LRP)

The work of the magician often begins with the pentagram or more precisely the Lesser Ritual of the Pentagram or its equivalent. Almost every serious ritualist knows it. You can go most places in the world and transcend any language barrier with this rite. Even so its origin are a bit of a puzzle. The ritual first appeared in instructional papers on the Pentagram for the outer order of the Golden Dawn. Expert Nick Farrell writes that in the original papers, the *invoking* version was much more prominent than its *banishing* counterpart. In the so-called "lesser version" the magician traces pentagrams in each of the cardinal directions. The elemental quality of these symbols is determined by one's starting point and direction. Hence the lower left or fifth point of an upright pentagram is said to correspond with the Earth element. The topmost corresponds with Spirit. If you trace the pentagram beginning from Spirit anti-clockwise or *widdershins*, it is said to be invoking. On the other hand, should one need a banishing, one begins at the Earth point and proceeds in a clockwise or *deosil* direction.

---

22   Nick Farrell "In Defence of the Lesser Invoking Pentagram" Published in the *Hermetic Virtues Magazine*, Volume 2, Issue 3.

clockwise: invoking

anti-clockwise: banishing

Many post-Golden Dawn groups habitually use the banishing version, probably much more often than was originally intended. I must admit if I am asked to perform this ritual, I habitually favour the banishing version. However *intention* is probably more important than these subtle differences in technique. Even so what Nick Farrell says has persuaded me to think again.

The magicians of the Golden Dawn perhaps used the older Heptagram rite which they divided into two distinct parts. This Heptagram ritual is the precursor to the Pentagram and another Victorian ritual, the Hexagram. The *Heptagram* literaly means "seven characters" or sevenfold rite. A Khemetic Golden Dawn reinstates the older sevenfold version based on Egyptian sources.

The Heptagram originates in an ancient papyrus, part of the library of a magician from Thebes in ancient Egypt.[23] This library re-emerged in the

---

23.   Hans Dieter Betz (1986) *Greek Magical Papyri in Translation: including Demotic spells*, Chicago, intro

19th century and was translated into several European languages, as well as Latin. All these sources would have been available to MacGregor Mathers, the senior adept who compiled much of the Golden Dawn ritual material from sources in the British Library etc.

THE HEPTAGRAM

Magick can be surprisingly physical. Before starting this kind of ritual it is a good idea to do a gentle *physical* warm-up; ie., all of your muscles from top to bottom. Begin with gentle neck rolls; loosen your shoulders, hips, thighs, knees and feet and anything else that needs doing.

This ritual is powerful and was used by magicians of ancient Egypt and transcribed in the Theban's magical library. I like to preface this with an exercise similar in intent to the Golden Dawn *Middle Pillar* but derived from another manuscript in the "House of Life" at Abydos. This is published in *Papyrus Salt*.[24] I refer to this as the *Abydos Arrangement*:

Face North and visualise the constellation
Ursa Major. Draw down its power

Now turn to the East and say:
"Guardians of the House of Life at ....

Before me in the East: Nephthys
Behind me in the West Isis
On my right hand in the South is Set
And on my left hand, in the North Horus
For above me shines the body of Nuit
And below me extends the ground of Geb

---

24.   Lucie Lamy (1981) *Egyptian Mysteries: new light on the ancient knowledge*, Thames & Hudson. *Le Papyrus Salt 825* (B.M. 10051) : rituel pour la conservation de la vie en Égypte par Philippe Derchain (1964)

And in my centre abideth the 'Great Hidden God'. "

This action roots one at the crossroads of the four cardinal directions. But also the three planes: the earth, the sky and the centre. One stands at a point of equipose between them. This sphere of operation is sevenfold; seven is one of the most sacred and potent numbers in the magical tradition.

Before we consider the Khemetic Heptagram, I want to take a short diversion into the topic of sound within the Egyptian magical tradition.

VOWEL SONG

"It is highly significant, albeit extraordinary; that the device of the seven vowels was taken up in Demotic spells." [24]

"They employ the seven vowels, which they utter in due succession as the sound of these letters is so euphonious that men listen to it in preference to the flute or lyre." [25]

The above and other antique sources inform us that in Egypt, the priests sang hymns and incantations in praise of their Gods. The number seven was always considered extremely powerful by Egyptian magi. "Vowel song", using the seven sounds, is in many ways beyond any particular

---

24. Jacco Dieleman (2005)*Priests, tongues, and rites : the London-Leiden magical manuscripts and translation in Egyptian ritual (100-300 CE) Leiden : 66.*
25. Demetrius *On Style 71* quoted in J Dieleman (2005: 65)

language. It is part of the universal or international language of magick. We can also say that the nature of the vowels depends upon the structure of the human body, especially the vocal chords. Vowels *are* the sounds of nature. We can follow this idea backwards to the beginning of time or sideways into for example Hinduism, which also utilises "vowel song" in its science of mantra - the most famous example being the ancient mantra *Om*. Vowel song can become a freeform or improvised technique.

An ancient Gnostic composed the following polyphonic chant in which the congregation takes on the form of seven heavenly choirs:

> "The first heaven utters the Alpha, the one after it Epsilon, the third Eta, the fourth, which is in the middle of the seven, utters the force (or sound) of Iota, the fifth Omicron, the sixth Upsilon, and the seventh, which is the fourth from the middle, expresses the Omega ... All these powers, he says, when lined to one another, sound forth the praises of him by whom they were brought forth. The glory of this sound is sent up again to the Forefather. The echo of this utterance of praise is brought down to earth, according to him, and becomes the shaper and parent of the things on earth."[26]

In ancient Egypt words were sacred. Any word is both a sign representing something but also a sound. Scholars say that the very first Egyptian hieroglyphs were very like those images seen in dreams.[27] The

---

26. Quoted in David Frankfurter, "The magic of writing and the writing of magic: the power of the word in Egyptian and Greek traditions" *Helios - Journal of the Classical Association of the Southwest*, vol 21, no 2: 101

27. Jan Assmann (1987) *Moses the Egyptian : the memory of Egypt in western monotheism*, Harvard: 113

hieroglyphs are direct images of reality, with the proviso that reality for the ancient Egyptians included the otherworld of dreams. Not surprisingly, the Egyptians were among the very first known interpreters of dreams. Some of the earliest examples of dream manuals come from their temple libraries.

Greek magick, also popular in Egypt, was heavily influenced by the cult of Orpheus. Therefore some say it values sound over and above the signs or letters by which it is represented. The letters do service to the underlying sound which is seen as more archaic and primary. From the time of Cleopatra (69-30BCE) both magical systems began to coalesce. Even predominantly Greek spells show evidence of an Egyptian user and vice versa.[28]

Returning again to the example of the seven vowels of magick. The ancient Egyptian language had its own vowels but, as in Hebrew, did not use any special characters to represent them. In this sense the vowels of the Egyptian tongue are *hidden* or secret.[29]

The Egyptian and Greek vowels must have been similar. In Cleopatra's time, the native Egyptian priests embraced the seven Greek vowels. In fact the Greek vowels were themselves derived from a common fund of Semitic semi-vowels (eg: Y becoming I) including those of the ancient Egyptian tongue.

---

28. Dielemann (2005 : 146). Recent research has revealed that even the ancient Pyramid texts paid some attention to correct vocalisation - see Baines - lecture
29. E Doblhofer (1961 : 34) *Voices in stone : the decipherment of ancient scripts and writings*, London

These seven vowels can be seen as the 'soul' of the alphabet. These entities have power on many different levels. They are letters, numbers and musical notes. They and indeed the consonants, correspond with the twenty-five notes of the Lute, the seven fold musical scale, etc., etc.

My book *Tankhem* suggests a mnemonic device by which one can easily remember the seven vowels:

Father Get Game to Feed the Hot New Home.

So for example to vocalise A, sing the word "Father", repeat a couple of times with the emphasis on the A in Father. Next drop everything apart from the A, and you have the vowel.

The seven sacred vowels:

Alpha :	α	A	A
Epsilon :	ε	E	E
Eta :	η	H	Ê
Iota :	ι	I	I
Omicron :	o	O	O
Upsilon :	υ	Υ	U
Omega :	ω	Ω	Ô

Character name, then lower case, upper case and Roman transliteration respectively.

CARDINALITY

Combinations of these vowels are used to invoke the divine forces of the four directions. For some these correspond to the four elements - earth, air, fire and water. David Rankine and Sorita D'Este write that the "alchemist Zosimos of Panopolis [in Egypt] attributed the elements to the four cardinal points in his classic third century work "Upon the Letter Omega". The attribution of the four elements to the four directions remained constant for many centuries, with Fire in the east, Air in the south, Water in the west and Earth in the north. This can be seen through to at least the Eighteenth century, where the *Key of Solomon* records that, "the spirits created of fire are in the East and those of the winds in the South . . . It would be Eliphas Levi in the mid 19th century with his writings who clearly switched the attributions of Air and Fire, giving Air as being attributed to the East and Fire to the South . . . This attribution was picked up by the Hermetic Order of the Golden Dawn, and has become the standard attribution in nearly all of the Western Esoteric Traditions."[30]

CARDINAL WINDS

If, as I do, you prefer a more wholely Egyptian presentation of the cardinal directions, then you might like to use another schema of four primary winds - ruled over by Shu, the God of the atmosphere, the air and winds.

---

30. David Rankine and Sorita D'Este (2008) *Practical Elemental Magick*, Avalonia

The winds are -

North = Meheyet: Ram headed winged lion

East = Iabet: Scarab with four rams' heads, yellow, also left side

West = Jimenet, Blue. Ram headed falcon with four wings.
Also symbolises the right side.

South = Resey: Lion with four rams heads and four wings.

This ritual is given in liturgical form elsewhere. I am repeating it here in order to analyse its components.

The Heptagram (sevenfold) rite combines physical gesture with intonation, vibrating or singing of words of power.

The first gesture is called "Horus Fighting". Inhale and in one perfect movement, form both hands into fists and raise them up and to the left of your head.

Next stretch your right hand and arm in front of you and bring the left hand and arm to join it. As you finish the intonation, bring both hands back to the centre of your body. [You'll be glad you did the physical warmup recommended earlier!]

Combine the above gesture with the first vowel long and hard - AAAAAAA -

Now starwise, ie turn anticlockwise or widdershins stopping at direction North. Most antique systems move in the directions of the stars.

Again make the gesture "Horus Fighting" and vibrate the second vowel EEEEEEE, using the mnemonic gEt as above.

Then turn to the West
Make the "Horus Fighting" gesture and vibrate ÊÊÊÊÊÊÊ as in GAme

Turn to the South
Make the "Horus Fighting" gesture and vibrate IIIIIII as in fEEd

Return to face the East
Now bend over and reach down to the Earth
vibrating OOOOOOO as in HOt

The second body magick posture is similar to one known as the Typhon or Trident in the Golden Dawn system. Combined with the Horus Fighting posture, it is very like a popular sequence of yogic postures known as Sun Salutation.

One begins from a loose forward bend, knees flexed and not locked, touching the earth. It does have a tendency to induce gentle shaking, especially in the lower legs. This is useful. Shaking helps focus the mind.

Gradually unfold, come up and place your hands on your heart and vibrate YYYYYYY as in NEw

Finally stretching up to the heavens vibrate Ô Ô Ô Ô Ô Ô Ô as in HÔme.

To finish I suggest a final welcoming of the principal Gods invoked by the rite. It's an odd fact that when one uses simple combinations of vowels, one is spontaneously speaking the ancient Egyptian magical language (More of this later). Make the invoking sign of the pentagram in the air in front of you and vibrate this sequence of vowels:

Aa, Eye, EE, Ou, Uh[30] - Nephthys
Continue thus:

Aa, Eye, EE, Ou, Uh Horus
Aa, Eye, EE, Ou, Uh Isis
Aa, Eye, EE, Ou, Uh Set
Aa, Eye, EE, Ou, Uh Geb
Aa, Eye, EE, Ou, Uh Nuit
Aa, Eye, EE, Ou, Uh Hidden God

---

30. Ay EAO - in Middle Egyptian this could mean "Oh Hail" - as it is a suitable piece of "magical voice" at the beginning of a line.

Repeat first part that begins "Guardians of the House etc."

Return to the North

After that preliminary rite - settle down - prepare for a short vision quest or visualisation - sit down in a posture suitable for meditation - this is your *asana* - it does not need to be uncomfortable to be effective. In the later Hindu tradition one is recommended to use a posture that is easy and comfortable.[31] The important thing is that your back is upright and neither tense nor slumped, perhaps *poised* is the right term.

When I first learnt this technique I was told to close my eyes and think about the room or place - recalling how it looked to the front - behind - to the sides. With my imagination I visualised a curtain in the east. As I "looked" (my eyes still closed) the curtain had an image on it - an equal armed cross - white on dark ground. This was then augmented with four *elemental* colours taken from the "King" scale from the sphere of Malkuth (the Kingdom) - the realm of earth hence the earthy or natural colours citrine, olive, russet and black.[32] Whilst the above exercise is still valid what follows is more *khemetically* focused version.

THE DOOR

Begins in a similar way to above but the image on the cloth is different. It is the "false door" mentioned earlier (see frontispiece illustration). It has proved a useful piece of magical technology. Indeed it is worth

---

31. *Yoga Sutras of Patanjali* - 2.46 "asana is steady, stable and comfortable" - the *Bhagavad Gita* has more detail at 6:13.

32. See *The Qabbalah of Aleister Crowley including 777.*

taking some time to make one of these as a canvas backdrop. I move mine around but it could hang behind what I'd call the offering table. Its portable nature means it can also be folded away when not in use. I will explain the meaning of the term "offering table" later.

This particular version of the false door is painted in matt white on a deep black background. This combination of black and white has a particular effect on consciousness. This use of contrasting colours, whether mono or polychrome is one of the important insights, perhaps even "secrets" of the Golden Dawn and is directly related to the colour theories of the ancient Egyptians.

The earliest form of the Egyptian tomb was a simple burial pit. The earliest brick built *mastabas* (from Arabic meaning "bench") augmented this pit with chambers for offerings and grave goods but then also surrounded it with symbolic doors. Later structures extend the theme but in essence there are two spaces, the chamber with burial shaft for the body. This chamber is sealed after the funeral and is then approached via a chapel, often open to the elements, but obviously designed to facilitate the visitation of living family members. The surviving relatives and friends visit the tomb to re-supply, to clean and to *continue* their relationship with their departed. This is ancestor worship - and as such is probably one of the oldest forms of religious activity.

Illustrated is another very early example from the Old Kingdom cemetary of the Giza pyramid field, probably 6th dynasty circa 2300BCE. My modern redrawn version is based on these ancient Egyptian examples. The connection between these spaces, one for the living, the other for the dead continues via the symbolic door; for this reason it is known by

Figure 4.6. Studio Photograph of the False Door Niche, MFA 21.961, Showing the Incorrect Reconstruction of the Left Outer Jamb (Containing the 𓂝 sign). Courtesy of the Museum of Fine Arts, Boston

"The Giza Mastaba Niche and Full Frontal Figure of Redi-Nes in Museum of Fine Arts, Boston" - Peter der Manuellian (1994) in *For His Ka: Essays in Memory of Klaus Baer*, 1994). There is a very early example of Queen Neithhotep of 1st dynasty, and found at Nagada by Jacques de Morgan.

archaeologists as the "false" or "*Ka*" door. The term "false door" is misleading - it is not really false, it is merely impassable for the living.

The Egyptians divided a person into several spiritual componants or *souls*. The *Ka* is one of these parts, is a spirit, and was able to pass through these doors with ease. Communication can be initiated by either party to the door. When the dead initiate the connection this can be a problem and the living need to beware! [33]

MORE ON THAT "FALSE" DOOR

Despite a door's commonplace nature it is well worth taking some time to re-acquaint yourself with its symbolism. In some senses when all else crumbles to dust, the doorway is often the last thing to disappear. The temples of Egypt are nowadays a shadow of their former selves, a glorious remnant. We moderns are the successors to the mysterious adepts who in the third century of our era (c268CE) prophesised Egypt's vertiginous fall but also its eventual resurgence.

> ". . .Egypt is an image of heaven or, to be more precise, that everything governed and moved in heaven came down to Egypt, and was transferred there? If truth were told, our land is the temple of the whole world. . .Oh Egypt, of your reverent deeds only stories will survive and they will be incredible to your children! Only words

---

33. Emily Teeter (2011) *Religion and ritual in ancient Egypt*, CUP : 48 "contact could be initiated by either side . . . The messages from the living were usually practical rather than philosophical. Less controlled, and hence more dangerous, were the messages initiated by the dead."

cut in stone will survive to tell your faithful works, and
. . . strangers will dwell [here]. . . no one will look up to
heaven. The reverent will be thought mad, the irreverent
wise, the lunative will be thought brave and the scoundrel
will be taken for a decent person. When all this has come
to pass . . . then the master and father, the God whose
power is primary, governor of the first God, will look on
this conduct and these willful crimes, and in an act of
will he will take his stand against the vices . . . he will
restore the world in its beauty of old so that the world
itself will again seem deserving of worship and wonder
. . . this will be the geniture of the world, the reformation
of all good things and a restitution, most holy and most
reverent, of nature itself." [34]

Existentially we stand outside the still ruined temple, literally on the
threshold, thus the image of the door is entirely appropriate. It is certainly
no coincidence that many books of the European Occult Renaissance
had on the frontispiece the image of a door, the portal to the secrets in
the book. The history of Pagans and books are intertwined. The book
as we know is very much a creation of the ancient Pagan world. Even
the familiar shape of the book conceals the Pythagorian "Golden Mean".
One of the most famous examples of a Renaissance Hermetic book is
John Dee's Elizabethan masterpiece, the *Monas Hieroglyphica.*

---

34. *The Asclepius* verses 24-27, translation by B P Copenhaver *The Greek
Hermetica* CUP 1992 p 81-2

I doubt I have exhausted the ramifications of this image. Everyone who sees it finds in it new connotations. For example some see the Hebrew "Cheth", the twin pillars and lintel upon which the ancient Hebrews daubed magical signs in lamb's blood to prevent the angel of death entering.

Others see something resembling the trilithon of ancient British megalithic architecture:

Take another look at the image of the false door that appears on the frontispiece. It would be a good idea to make your own copy at a good size and place this where it can be glimpsed during ritual. I have one on the wall opposite my bed. It is often the last thing I see before I fall asleep. This complies with the advice found in the books of Dion Fortune that the adept should "sleep" within the astral temple. This is an important magical instruction especially for those working within the Khemetic tradition where dreams and the dreamscape are the primary theatre of magick. A great many Khemetic ritual techniques are completed in dreams: hence if one invokes a God they are invariably expected to respond via a dream. This is an important technique on which there will be more to say a little later.

But for the moment the rite has begun with the basic opening liturgy and the initiate lingers before a representation of the false door that is the portal to greater mysteries. From its beginnings in early tombs and *mastabas* the door was soon incorporated into the design of temples. The first temples were temporary structures. One of the earliest known is from circa 4000BCE in the abandoned settlement of Hierakonpolis, which means "Citadel of the Hawk." The Egyptian name *Nekhen* links this with the followers of the God Horus and the conflicts that supposedly led at the very beginning of Egyptian formal history, to unification or hegemony of one local tribe over another.

Above is a provisional reconstruction of this proto-shrine deduced from the post holes and foundations. The structure appears temporary and at a push could well have been relocated. It recalls an earlier, more nomadic lifestyle when shrines were portable. Its shape is said to be modelled on the body of a large animal - probably a bull but other *preformal* structures also recall the body of a wolf. It seems likely that early treatment of the deceased involved what's come to be known as 'sky-burial' - i.e. exposure to the elements and the teeth of wild animals such as wolves.

These temples share some of the symbology of a tomb. Inside there were two nested rooms, an outer *peristyle* and an inner holy of holies. This structure is pretty much the same as the arrangement of the temple as discussed earlier in connection with the medieval *Book of Abramelin*.

A palisade surrounded the entire shrine forming the *temenos* or sacred enclosure. The temenos of the temple of Medinet Habu is intact and still inspires in me a spontaneous sense of awe. Within the temenos stood a large pole from which fluttered a sacred image. The front end of the shrine was supported on four masts, perhaps also surmounted by fetishes, flags or streamers. The motif of four masts or pillars at the front of a shrine was often repeated in subsequent religious buildings, the most obvious being the shrines seen in the enclosure attached to the Pyramid of Djozer at Saqqara. In Egyptian "Kabbalah" the number four signifies completeness (qv).

These early buildings can be read as complete models of the ancient cosmos. It is another of those "mind maps" left by our distant ancestors. As soon as they acquired writing they recorded these ancient secrets in books such as the aptly titled 'The Book of the Primeval Old Ones'.[35]

It "tells that in the primeval times the surface of the planet was covered with water. Below the water lay the remains of one or more previous creations. The divine entities were without form but not without power. The ancient sages or *shamans* call out to these beings, using words of power that they had but recently learnt. There are . . .seven sages [there's

---

35. E A R Reymond (1969) *The Mythological Origin of the Egyptian Temple*, Manchester.

that number seven again] or shamans and this is another motif that seems to crop up all over the place. This is, in all likelihood, the origin of the myth of Atlantis." [36]

The result is the first and most primal temple, built or moved to the new dry land. The divine entities arrange themselves at the four cardinal points as well as above, below and centre, precisely as spoken in the first part of the sevenfold *Heptagram* rite discussed earlier. When you meditate before the first version of the temple all of this knowledge is manifest plus much more to come.

The tented shrine was the first formal entrance to the numinous, and the Underworld. In ancient times the Egyptian architect Imhotep recreated this cosmic model in stone, reifying the mysteries into the structure of the archetypal Egyptian temple. Imhotep was over time viewed as a God because of his expertise. As time went by the details became increasingly obscure and complex. In essence a temple is a mechanism by which we can return to the source, the primary moment of equipoise, ecstacy and eternity.

Sometimes we need the complexities of the temple, sometimes we need something simpler.

GREEK VOWELS AND THE ELEMENTS?

If, like me you were brought up in the Western mystery tradition then you may be wondering whether there is any correspondence between these vowels and the four or five magical elements of earth, air, fire,

---

36. See Morgan *Tankhem* page 54

water and spirit? The liturgy at the end of this book, provides a revised version of an opening (*Heptagram*) rite based on a text in the *Theban Magical library*.[37] In this ritual the magician intones (*vibrates*) the seven sacred vowels in the following order:

Alpha	-	East
Epsilon	-	North
Eta	-	West
Iota	-	South
Omicron	-	Below
Upsilon	-	Centre
Omega	-	Above

Egyptian Gods and Goddesses are commonly arranged into similar patterns. The "Abydos Arrangement" discussed earlier is one such example. Another common ancient arrangement used the four Goddesses Mut-Sekhmet-Bastet-Wadjet.[38] One can therefore deduce correspondences between the vowel sounds and the Gods.

CARMINA FIGURATA

As well as chanting vowels, the Egyptian mage wrote them on amulets, often arranging them in patterns to re-emphasise the power of the written word - hence the name "carmina figurata" - *shaped hymns*. There were three principal patterns, each comprising seven tiers. The patterns are triangle or square or diamond, the later also known as a wing (pterugion).

---

37. PGM XIII verses 823-835
38. Richard Jasnow & Mark Smith " 'As for Those Who have Called me Evil, Mut will Call them Evil': Orgiastic Cultic Behaviour and its Critics in Ancient Egypt" *Enchoria: Zeitschrift für Demotistik und Koptologie* Band 32 2010/2011 : 25

Further variations are available according to whether the triangle or pyramid points up or down and also how the seven vowels appear in the tiers.

These squares are called *plinthion:*

```
a  a  a  a  a  a  a
e  e  e  e  e  e  e
è  è  è  è  è  è  è
i  i  i  i  i  i  i
o  o  o  o  o  o  o
y  y  y  y  y  y  y
ô  ô  ô  ô  ô  ô  ô


a  e  è  i  o  y  ô
e  è  i  o  y  ô  a
è  i  o  y  ô  a  e
i  o  y  ô  a  e  è
o  y  ô  a  e  è  i
y  ô  a  e  è  i  o
ô  a  e  è  i  o  ô
```

Thus one is called a wing (*Pterugion*)

```
a  e  è  i  o  y  ô
   e  è  i  o  y  ô  a
      è  i  o  y  ô  a  e
         i  o  y  ô  a  e  è
            o  y  ô  a  e  è  i
               y  ô  a  e  è  i  o
                  ô  a  e  è  i  o  ô
```

The vowels may be multiplied for example tripled for extra emphasis or written in exponential form [39] –

a

e e

è è è

i i i i

o o o o o

y y y y y

ô ô ô ô ô ô ô

When we use these techniques, either drawing or intoning them as sound *shapes*, we are following in the footsteps of our Egyptian ancestors. And as we are eclectic, so too were they, incorporating new words of power, such as ABRASAX, into the system. Egyptian magick is in no way purist.

---

39. PGM I 1-42

"IN PRAISE OF NONSENSE" EPHESIAN LETTERS[40]

From "vowel song" it is an easy step to the distinctive international code of antique magic, the so-called "*Voce Magicae*". Aleister Crowley coined the phrase "barbarous words of invocation". These were also called "Ephesian grammata" or "Ephesian letters". These were additional letters that had power over and above the sounds they represented.[41] Ephesus was at this time a byword for exotic practice and incantation. These strange word and sound patterns are an essential part of any effective invocation. From the improvised, freeform recitation of vowels, some memorable sound patterns naturally emerge.

LUSCIOUS SYLLABLES

These sound pattern favour so-called "luscious syllables". This is the Orphic, musical side of magick. A perennial favourite in the magical literature of the centuries after the death of Cleopatra is:

ABLANATHANALBA

Which was usually invoked for beneficient results, and often occuring in conjunction with:

SESENGENBARPHARANGES.

or

AKRAMMACHAMARA

---

40. "In Praise of Nonsense" quoted in Frankfurter WoM fn 83 Patricia Cox Miller in *Classical Mediterranean spirituality: Egyptian, Greek, Roman* ed by A H Amstrong (NY 1986) 481-505

41 David Frankfurter (1998) *Religion in Roman Egypt* Princeton page 195

The meaning is unexplained but some say it contains Hebrew.[42] Another common "luscious" invocation was "DAMNAMENEUS" - which wouldn't be out of place in the pages of a Harry Potter novel!

The sound here is more important than any meaning. Although when written on amulets, the Egyptian doctrine of hieroglyphs is again revealed, for this sound pattern then gets a visual shape such as those used in the vowels eg: here it is as a "wing". In this magick both aspects, sound and image, constantly interchange one with another. The sound pattern becomes a visual thing - the visual becomes sound. This is *synesthesia.*

ABLANATHANALBA

BLANATHANALBA

LANATHANALBA

ANATHANALBA

NATHANALBA

ATHANALBA

THANALBA

HANALBA

ANALBA

NALBA

ALBA

LBA

BA

A

Now this magical or artificial language takes on a life of its own - or maybe the life was there all the time but we had forgotten how to see it. This happened to the Egyptian magicians - who started using this artificial

---

42.   Betz (1986) page 331

language as an "alphabetic demotic" – preserving but also unintentionally hiding ancient Egyptian God names and epithets.[43]

Our modern perspective is not so different to that of the clients of the ancient mages whose spells were often done for their benefit, even if they did not really understand what was going on. The priests performed direct rituals and acted vicariously on behalf of their clients. Socrates wrote in his dialogue *Charmides* [44] that "without the spoken formula the leaf [spell] has no power". But they also devised many visual and other techniques with "concrete" efficacy; for example the famous "drinking and eating spells" described in numerous places, including my book *The Bull of Ombos*. Amulets may also function as spoken utterances of a God.

There is an interesting contemporary use of this technique in Nick Farrell's book *Making Talismans*. To rid oneself of a boil, write the word thus:

BOIL
BOI
BO
B

"TWILIGHT LANGUAGE"

Magicians of all times have felt the need for secrecy. In late antiquity codes and euphemisms were used to disguise the socially unacceptable componants of a working. In some spells, for example those to send

---

43.   Dielemann (2005 : 73)
44.   155E

"evil sleep", the coded sections tells how the spell repeated seven times will kill the intended victim. One possible counter-measure is to block dreams entirely and this is one of the known side-effects of the narcotic blue lily potion discussed elsewhere and widely used by ancient Egyptian specialists. Even so, dreamless sleep is difficult to guarantee!

Use of private languages is also partly about preserving professional mystique. The Egyptians did this via an institution known as the "House of Life", a restricted archive of manuscripts attached to every temple. Secrecy also persisted beyond life, with some texts only known from copies deposited in tombs. There were also books inscribed on the walls of sealed rooms in temples such as Sety I at Abydos. These are ancient Egyptian *Books of the Afterlife* never discussed in other Egyptian records.[45]

Egyptian hieroglyphics is such a complex language it was easy to veil precise meanings by omitting a grammatical element. For example the determinative, a little picture that tells you the context of a word and without which the word has several often conflicting meanings. This is known as *enigmatic writing*. Another twilight language is called *acrophany*, where a particular sound is expressed by means of another common word, of which only the first consonant or syllable has phonetic relevance.[46] A classic example is "Never Eat Shredded Wheat", not that that you shouldn't, just happens to be a handy way to remember the cardinal directions: North, South, East, West. We also call this mnemonics and it is a common part of magick.

---

45.   E Hornung (1999) *The Ancient Egyptian Books of the Afterlife*, Cornell
46.   Dielemann (2005 : 78)

Back in the day, the magician was supposed to know the basics, the things already discussed but also special formulae such as the MASKELL –MASKELLO. This obscure phrase is really just the first two words of a much longer spell containing crucial words of power. [47]

"SIGILS" - THE NEW HIEROGLYPHS

From the uneasy, arranged marriage of the two magical cultures was forged a new alternative to the hieroglyphs, incorporating elements of the Greek and Egyptian language. These are the so-called "charaktêres". The charaktêres are freeform signs (Latin 'sigils') used as an alternative to hieroglyphs at a time when knowledge of them was becoming lost or attenuated due to official Greek indifference. These signs were still in use on 17th century magical gems and remain effective tools. [48]

Thus the well-known neo-Pagan rite, the Bornless or Headless ritual, made famous by the Order of the Golden Dawn and after that by Aleister Crowley, uses an ancient charaktêre.

---

47. Betz (1986 : 336) PGM IX . 10, XXXVI 342
48. Cambell-Bonner Magical Gem Database, EA 56360A, 17th century gem shows Christ-Osiris with Greek words and charaktêres. See also Kirsten Dzwiza http://www.charakteres.com

The above transcription may differ from some published versions but is taken directly from the standard reference edition of the text.[49] Sometimes a spell has just one sigil or charaktêre, sometimes whole groups are given, suggesting they represented complex words and sentences.

Another name for this ritual is the "Ritual of Jeu the Hieroglyphist" or "painter of Hieroglyphs". This is a very significant name, perhaps related to *Jesus* or *Jahweh*. He or she may have been a famous practitioner of his time, and even if they didn't actually write this spell, they provided a powerful "brand" . Amongst Egyptian books re-discovered in our time are the so-called Nag Hammadi "gospels". This cache included several Hermetic texts such as *The Books of Jeu*. Amongst the diagrams is a remarkable survival of Egyptian Hieroglyphic - the famous Ankh symbol morphed into the Gnostic/Christian Khi-Rho.[50]

49.   K Preisendanz (1928-41) *Papyri Graecae Magica*, Teubner.

50.   *The Books of Jeu and the untitled text in the Bruce codex text* ed. by Carl Schmidt ; translated [from the Coptic] Leiden : Brill 1978

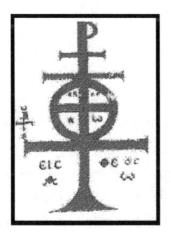

SEVEN CHARAKTÊRES FOR "DELIVERANCE"

The total number of charactêres is very large. The first draft of this book made an arbitrary choice of the first seven as they appeared in the Theban magical library. However, I subsequently discovered that my idea was very similar to the "seven seals" of medieval Islamic magick, which is semitic magick ultimately derived from Cuneiform and Mesopotamian sources. Most of us know that during the European "Dark Ages" medieval Islam preserved a great deal of ancient learning. Many magical ideas actually come down to us via this route. The great Islamic sorcerer Al Buni believed the seven seals to be a blend of Hebrew, Islamic and Christian symbolism. Thus the first two seals were, so he says, from the *Koran*, seals 3 & 4 are from the *New Testament* and the final three are from the *Torah*.

To my eye they look older than any of those sources, indeed very much like ancient Egyptian *heiratic* script and some support for this conclusion comes from independent Islamic scholar Lloyd D Graham.[51]

For magicians unfamiliar with Islamic sorcery one's first encounter with the seven seals would probably be via the final book of the *New Testament* (chapters 5-9). This is a magical, apocalyptic text written in the reign of Roman Emperor Domitian (1st century CE) by a mystic who identifies himself as John, an exile on the Greek island of Patmos. Elaine Pagels, the esteemed scholar of Gnosticism says this is a political text, a cryptic attack on the despotic Roman hegemony. This fact is not to deny the presence of ancient magick in the text. The text is very well-known but here are some of the relevant verses:

> *5.1:* And I saw in the right hand of him that sat on the throne a book written within and on the backside, sealed with seven seals.

Unlike other magical texts the seven seals are not shown in any extant manuscript thus far found. However one does encounter what must be equivalent seals almost as soon as one looks at any magical "grimoire" or papyrus of the late classical period. Hence PGM I 262-347 says that to invoke the Sun God Apollo "take a seven-leafed sprig of laurel and hold it in your right hand / as you summon the heavenly Gods and chthonic daimons. Write on the sprig of laurel the seven charactêres for deliverance."

---

51. "The Seven Seals of Judeo-Islamic Magic, possible origins of the symbols" published in www.academic.edu.com

The spell in question actually then shows eight charaktêres, which makes me think the phrase "seven charaktêres of deliverance" is either a stock or generic phrase or, as happens in later examples, the first, and perhaps most important seal is repeated.

The seven seals are :

7 6 5 4 3 2 1

(a)　　　　　　　　　　Islamic

1st Seal: The Pentagram

> "*6.1:* And I saw when the Lamb opened one of the
> seals, and I heard, as it were the noise of thunder, one
> of the four beasts saying, Come and see.
> *6.2:* And I saw, and behold a white horse: and he that
> sat on him had a bow; and a crown was given unto
> him: and he went forth conquering, and to conquer."

The series is to be read right to left. The first of these is the pentagram. In modern magick the inverted pentagram is usually thought of as "satanic". Both kinds are known from medieval magick. Lloyd Graham examined 58 examples and found that the downward pointing variation occured in 15 of these; which suggests the downward pointing is rarer and perhaps always did have a different meaning.[52]

The sequence of seven in ancient religion is perhaps related to a primary constellation of the seven most powerful Gods and their seven powerful adversaries. The actual stellar counterpart would be the constellation of the Pleiades for most of Mesopotamia; Ursa Major for Egypt.

This pentagram symbol is very old, it occurs for instance on pottery as an ancient predynastic maker's or owner's mark. For certain technical reasons is seems likely that the asterisk-like symbol shown below is an alternative version of the pentagram. As a word it is pronounced "An" in ancient Sumerian and means sky or heaven. It was used to introduce the name of a God. Probably it is equivalent to Greek vowel Alpha.

---

52. Lloyd Graham, personal communication 2012 "Interesting question about the orientation of the pentagram. I've now looked at 58 representations of the Seven Seals and found the upwards orientation (i.e. single point at top) in 43 cases, downwards pointing (i.e. two points at top) in just 15 cases. So it seems that there is a strong bias against the "horns" orientation even in old inscriptions from Islamic lands. So perhaps the modern Western distinction between the two orientations has ancient roots."

53. See Lloyd Graham op cit p 4. See also Cambell-Bonner Database for two examples of pentagrams and asterisk star on talismanic gems.

In Egyptian hieroglyphic, words to do with stars, time etc are determined by a five pointed star.[54] I'd remind you that a pentagram can be formed by joining the arms of a five pointed star.

The asterisk form of this sigil is what finds its way into the medieval grimoires such as the *Key of Solomon*, where it is part of the design on the handle of a magical knife or *Athame* - and this turns up again in the Gardnerian *Book of Shadows*.

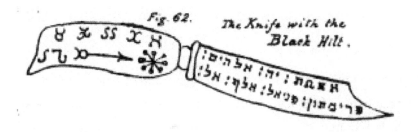

The point to remember is that the pentagram and its variant the asterisk is a very old hieroglyph. Its precise grammatical meaning may be lost but knowledge of its magical power endures. Perhaps it was always emotive, coming straight from the unconscious. The pentagram is said to be related to the fifth letter of the Arabic alphabet isolated *Ha* sound (*He* in Hebrew). Al Buni says this and second seal originate in the *Koran*.

---

54. N14 in the standard hieroglyphic sign list

2nd Seal

"6.3: And when he had opened the second seal, I heard the second beast say, Come and see. *4:* And there went out another horse that was red: and power was given to him that sat thereon to take peace from the earth, and that they should kill one another: and there was given unto him a great sword."

There is less to say about the second sigil. Ancient Arabic sorcerers saw the first letter of their alphabet (Alif), repeated three times. Al Buni says it is Koranic.

3rd Seal

"*6.5:* And when he had opened the third seal, I heard the third beast say, Come and see. And I beheld, and lo a black horse; and he that sat on him had a pair of balances in his hand."

If you rotate the third seal (*mem*) 90 degrees is does resemble a balance. It also looks like the Arabic letter mem (mim), perhaps "M" for Mohammed, although others cite a Biblical origin. Al Buni says it comes from the *New Testament* (Evangelists).

4th Seal

"*6.7:* And when he had opened the fourth seal, I heard the voice of the fourth beast say, Come and see. *8:* And I looked, and behold a pale horse: and his name that sat on him was Death, and Hell followed with him. And power was given unto them over the fourth part of the earth, to kill with sword, and with hunger, and with death, and with the beasts of the earth."

Some see a ladder in this seal, on which the blessed may ascend to heaven. It is also a box-grid of nine squares or chambers well known in Kabbalah. The central square is could also be the marking out of the fourth part of the earth that perishes under the hoofs of the fourth horseman! Al Buni says from the glyph is from *New Testament* (Evangelists).

5th Seal

"*6.9:* And when he had opened the fifth seal, I saw under the altar the souls of them that were slain for the word of God, and for the testimony which they held: *10:* And they cried with a loud voice, saying, How long, O Lord, holy and true, dost thou not judge and avenge our blood on them that dwell on the earth? *11:* And white robes were given unto every one of them; and it was said unto them, that they should rest yet for a little season, until their fellow servants also and their brethren, that should be killed as they were, should be fulfilled."

This sign occurs in amulets and is interpreted by some scholars as the Semitic letter *het* which is similar to the following Egyptian hieroglyph:[55]

The four strokes like four alifs could also be a reference to Tetragrammaton, the fourfold name of God. Four is also the number of Jupiter. Al Buni says its origins are in the *Torah*.

---

55. O42 in standard Egyptian signlist phonetically = Shesep, a fence outside a primitive shrine, ie the one that marks out the temenos. Lloyd Graham "The Seven Seals of Judeo-Islamic Magic, possible origins of the symbols"

6th Seal

> *"6.12:* And I beheld when he had opened the sixth seal,
> and, lo, there was a great earthquake; and the Sun became
> black as sackcloth of hair, and the Moon became as
> blood; *13:* And the stars of heaven fell unto the Earth,
> even as a fig tree casteth her untimely figs, when she is
> shaken of a mighty wind. *14:* And the heaven departed
> as a scroll when it is rolled together; and every mountain
> and island were moved out of their places."

Al Buni says this sign also originates from the *Torah*.[54] Other authorities
see in this sign a hand gesture or even a phallus.

---

56. "5,6,7, are from the Torah, 3 & 4 from the Gospel and 1 & 2 are from
the Koran" quoted in Hans Winkler (1930) *Siegel and charaktêre. in der
Mohammedanischen Zauberei* 80

The 7th Seal

"*8.1:* And when he had opened the seventh seal, there was silence in heaven about the space of half an hour. *2:* And I saw the seven angels which stood before God; and to them were given seven trumpets."

The Biblical text continues with the appearance of the seven angels with trumpets that sound to herald general death and destruction. It may also represent Arabic *waw* - which is the main conjunction in Arabic and when prefixed to some nouns gives them greater significance as in "I swear by". The seal might also represent the sound of those trumpets. Rotated 90° clockwise and it is an eye, benign, evil or eye of destruction! Destruction in Pagan thought is good and bad. Like the opening of the eye of Shiva, which sweeps away illusion along with much else, clearing the ground for something new in the world or within one's psyche.

Outside of a Christian Fundamentalist context, the *Book of Revelation* is an extraordinary example of a class of magical/apocalyptic texts of the late classical world. It is high magick, dealing with the ultimate *Gnostic* revelation. If my working hypothesis about these seals raises concerns about revealing too much dangerous knowledge, let me reasure you that something more is required for that. Despite all this drama, the later use of the seven seals is not invariable apocalyptic. They are used in different ways on charms with a wide range of intents. They are still widely used in the construction of magical squares as an alternative to the seven Greek vowels for example this power 7x7 and 8x8 amulets against misfortune (the first seal repeated at the end):

USAGE

So in summary, I've presented the seven most prominent charaktêres or seals from amongst hundred of others. The entire body of charaktêres are in effect the freeform magical language that developed in late classical Egypt. They are new, spontaneous hieroglyphs used in the magick of the time. You may find that these seven are the only that one really needs.

THE RING OF POWER

I was recently asked to work magick to bring someone prosperity and success in their chosen career. For this I used material from two linked manuscripts from the Theban magical library.[57] I was grateful for this opportunity as my own magical ring was a gift from another magician and didn't really require any additional work. I was provided with a rapid lesson in the magical power of such objects when I almost lost it. Those of you who have become attached to a wedding or engagement ring will know precisely how that feels. It's surprising how much emotion one invests in a ring. Maybe there is a warning there.

The author of the spell in the magical library wrote in the tongue of his or her Greek masters. Even so he often added a note to remind himself of the Egyptian original. The second spell is an alternative to the first and uses some but not all of its recipes.

This little ring is for success and favour and victory. "It", the opening lines of the spell tell us, "makes men famous and great and admired and rich as can be, or it makes possible friendships with suchlike men. The circlet is always yours [to use] justly and successfully for all purposes. It contains a first rate name."

Having consecrated [the ring], wear it when you are pure. "Pure" in this context is probably another reference to priestly i.e., magical activity. A "wab" or pure is a grade of (part-time) priests. Thus the instruction is to wear the ring when doing the work of Egyptian Gods (Theurgy).

---

57. See PGM XII 201-216 & 270-350 and Dielemann (2005 : 159)

Such a ring, so the spell tells us, will enable you to, "get whatever you want from anybody. Besides it calms the anger of master and kings. Wearing it, whatever you say to anyone, you will be believed, and you will be pleasing to everybody. Anybody can open doors and break chains and rocks, if he touches them with the stone, that is, the gem and says the name written below. It also works for exorcising hostile demons. Just give it [to one to wear, and the daimon will immediately flee.]"

Some of this is hype, but all in all it is a useful and common enough artefact for a magick worker. The contemporary magician can and indeed unconsciously already has learnt much from these rituals. The ritual begins with a list of ingredients and then progresses to the ritual proper. The preparation for the rite starts with acquisition of a suitable ring, ideally one with a semi-precious gem. If you buy one with an existing inscription such as a permutation of the seven seals, it will still need to be "opened" or consecrated.

A sky blue Jasper; or green Heliotrope is ideal for this spell. According to Pliny's *Natural History*, heliotrope is a green chalcedony with small spots of red jasper. The "classic" bloodstone is green jasper with red inclusions of iron oxide (red jasper). The name "heliotrope" comes from the Greek *Helios* meaning Sun and *trepein* meaning "to turn", an ancient notion about the manner in which the mineral reflects light. Both stones are amongst several we might recognize as having solar qualities or *correspondences*.

The example used in the spell was engraved with the "Ouroboros" serpent - a serpent swallowing its own tail. This symbol is widely used on talismanic gems and is found on Egyptian monuments such as in the Tomb of Tutankhamun.[58]

The "ouroboros" frames or encircles another image. These must have been magnificent and expensive objects. We also see here another way of "casting a circle". One of those snakes encircles the crescent Moon, with stars at either horn beside the name Helios. The Moon here is in the service of the Sun, being in the bright or "solar" part of the lunar month.

This ancient example from the British Museum shows the Ouroborus with the seven stars. The reverse shows Harpokrates, Hekate, & Chnoubis: [59]

In another ring the Ouroboros encircles the scarab beetle Kephra. This and the other ring designs are connected with the *young* Sun; the Sun at its freshest and most vigorous moment. In the Egyptian lunar calendar the Moon is similarly fresh when its first crescent appears on the second day of the month. For the Egyptians, the Sun, like the Moon, had a

---

58   Alexandre Piankoff (1962) *The Shrines of Tut-Ankh-Amon*, NY

59.   Campbell-Bonner Database of magical gems, Cbd 129

triple form. Khephra, the scarab beetle represents the youthful, rising Sun. Khephra means "to become". Ra as a falcon is the Sun God in his *prime*. And Tum, the Ram represents the *ageing* Sun, in his twilight years. And all three phases are mentioned in the ritual for "opening" or "initiating" the ring. [60]

The reverse side of the gem stone was also used to bear various names in hieroglyphics and other languages but always with a clear solar connection. Examples include Helios, ABRASAX and IAO SABAOTH. ABRASAX or ABRAXAS by numerology using its Greek spelling totals 365, and thus corresponds to the solar year as mentioned in several other spells.[61]

So you get the message - the solar imagery is reinforced, over and over again.

TIMINGS FOR SOLAR RITES:

The ring can be consecrated at dawn facing the rising Sun. In the book *Supernatural Assault in Ancient Egypt* there is a discussion of the importance of dawn (the *Duat*) as a key twilight in Egyptian magick. The cult of the Sun, and the continuation of its course is one of the two major concerns of Egyptian religion, surviving into the *Corpus*

---

60. Crowley's well known solar ritual "Liber Resh" follows its own internal logic. Its cardinal schema is based on four Gods listed on the XXVIth dynasty stele of Ankh f n Khonsu, found at Qurna, Luxor, the so-called "the Stele of Revealing" viz Ra, Tum, Kephri and Hathor. See the translation he commissioned from two fellow occultists and Egyptologists Alan Gardiner & Battiscombe-Gunn. see Aleister Crowley (1988) *The Holy Books of Thelema*, NY p 253.

61. See PGM IV 331-32, VIII 49, 611; XIII 156, 466

Hermetica. The other being the protection of the mysteries of Abydos – the cult centre of the God Osiris.[62]

I used a slightly different although equally authentic set of solar times. I did it three times each day at approximately the third, sixth and ninth hour of the Egyptian clock. These times have long be standardized to 9am, 12noon and 3pm. The threefold execution re-enforces the division of the Sun into three phases as dawn, midday and sunset.[63] The rite was repeated for fourteen days beginning when the Moon begins its third quarter.

The ritual occurs during the moon's fall or dark trimester. This period is often associated with Horus. It is also what we might call the moon's absence, or "seizure" and therefore sun's strength. "Solar" and "lunar" rites are almost always mutually exclusive. Rites to the Sun being more often done on the "dark nights". Malign rites tend to cluster in the full Moon or period of "white nights" and this also corresponds with ritual information I provided for the correspondence between the Egyptian God Seth and the full Moon and Horus, his antithesis, corresponding with the new Moon. [64]

It is recommended that the month be one in which the Moon is rising in Taurus, Virgo, Scorpio or Aquarius. When performing the consecration one is simultaneously to hold the ring (or object to be consecrated) in

62. See Iamblicus *De mysteriis VI*, 7, 282, see discussion of this in Jan Assmann, Lecture at the Ritual Dynamics and the Science of Ritual Conference, Heidelberg Sept-Oct 2008
63. These times pass into Christian liturgy as Terce, Sixt and None.
64. Radcliffe G Edmonds III "At the Seizure of the Moon: The absence of the Moon in the Mithras Liturgy" Noegel S, J Walker J and B Wheeler (eds) *Prayer, Magic and the Stars in Ancient and Late Antique World*, Penn State U Press.

the smoke of the burnt offering. In my garden there is currently a small shrine over the tomb of my pet cat Aleister, who is now an "Akh" or otherworld helper. The shrine has a small brick altar on which I burn candles and incense to him and also the spirit of other household pets who have passed over, including Shoni the lurcher. I place the ring in a small chamber covered with a skylight and place the burning frankincense and cake of light in this chamber. I can leave the ring *in situ* for the entire period of the consecration without fear that some passing beast will carry it away.

The original consecration required similar equipment; a pit in a holy place open to the sky or a clean, sanctified tomb orientated to the east. An altar or platform of wood of fruit trees was built over this upon which a white goose, three roosters and three pigeons were sacrificed and burnt to cinders. Cover these offerings with all sorts of incense, although elsewhere it says avoid frankincense. Libate the cinders with wine, honey, milk and saffron and hold the stone over the smoke for the invocation.

We can surmise that all of these ingredients have solar qualities. In modern practice animal sacrifice is mostly avoided and since the time of early 19th century magus Francis Barrett, appropriate incense has been thought sufficient. Or, if you follow the nostrums of *Liber AL* "The best blood is of the Moon monthly" and the burning of a infused "cake of light" is widely considered to be more effective than animal sacrifice.[65]

You need some appropriate words - the papyri give some very long examples that combine Hebrew, Greek and Egyptian elements. Using

---

65.   For instructions see *The Bull of Ombos*

current research here's a restored version in the "original" Egyptian idiom. This invocation is rather long but one soon gets used to it. Almost every line implies a philosophical attitude and in order for the spell to work you have to have satisfied yourself that you understand and agree with this implicit theology. So even if you never use this spell - reading it, especially as part of a meditational practice is an important spiritual exercise. I'll first set out the whole invocation and follow this with a discussion of what it means to me.

I've shortened this somewhat as I suspect that over time parts that were once instructions have become incorporated into the words of power. The vibe is an address to the Sun, both visible and symbolic, as the pivot of the whole celestial hierarchy. Thus:

1. An address to the triple Sun

I invoke and beseech the consecration,

O Gods of the heavens

O Gods under the earth

O Gods circling on the middle region from one womb

O masters of all the living and dead

O heedful in many necessities of Gods and men

O concealers of things now seen

O directors of Isis, Nemesis and Adrasteia

who spend every hour with you

O senders of fate who travel around the whole world

O commanders of the rulers

O exalters of the abased

O revealers of the hidden

O guides of the winds

O arousers of the waves

O bringers of fire at the appropriate time

O creators and benefactors of every race

O Lords and controllers of kings

come, benevolent ones, for the purpose for which I call you, as

benevolent assistants in this rite for my benefit.

[Feel free to add or improvise some additional magical names]

2. Assumption of the God form

I am an outflow of blood from the tomb of Osiris

[between] the palm trees

I am the faith found in men and I am he who declares the holy names,

who is unchanging, who came forth from the abyss.

I am the sacred Phoenix bird

I am Helios

I am the God whom no one sees or rashly names

I am Shu the sender of winds

I am Tefnut the fire

I am Geb the earth

I am Nuit the mother of the Gods

I am Osiris called water

I am Isis called dew

I am Seth who defeats Apophis

I am Nephthys called spring

I am Harpocrates who came forth from the eye of the Sun

I am an image resembling the true image

Therefore I beseech you

come as my helpers,

for I am about to call on the hidden and ineffable name, the forefather

of the Gods, overseer and lord of all"

3. Hymn to the Demiurge

"Come to me,

you from the four winds,

God, ruler of all

who has breathed spirits into men for life,

master of the good things in the world.

Hear me, Lord whose hidden name is ineffable.

The daimons, hearing it, are terrified -

the name is:

barbareich arsemphem-phrothou

and of it the Sun,

and also the earth.

hearing, rolls over.

Hades, hearing is shaken

rivers, sea, lakes, springs, hearing are frozen

rocks, hearing it are split

Heaven is your head; ether body

earth feet

and water around you ocean

O Agathos Daimon

You are Lord, the begetter and nourisher and increaser of all."

4. Hexametrical hymn to the Demiurge

Who molded the forms of the beasts of the Zodiac

Who found their routes

Who was the begetter of fruits?

Who raises up the mountains?

Who made the winds to hold to their annual tasks

What Aion nourishing an Aion rules the Aions?

One deathless God

You are the begetter of all and assign souls to all and control all,

King of the Aions and Lord

before who

mountains and plains

springs and rivers

valleys of earth

spirits and all things

High shining heaven

and every sea

trembles.

Lord, ruler of all, holy one

and master of all.

By your power the elements exist and all things come into being,

the route of the Sun and Moon,

of night and dawn

all things in air and earth and water and fire.

Yours is the eternal processional way of [heaven]

in which the seven lettered name is established for the harmony of

the seven sounds of the planets which utter their voices according to

the phases of the Moon.

You give wealth, good old age, good children, strength, food.

You Lord of life, ruler of the upper and lower realm,

whose justice is not thwarted,

whose glorious name the angels hymn,

who have truth that never lies,

hear me and complete for me this operation so that I may wear this

power in every place,

in every time, without being smitten or afflicted,

so as to be preserved intact from every danger

while I wear this power.

Yea lord, for to you,

the God in heaven,

all things are subject, and none of the daimons or spirits will oppose

me because I have called on your great name for the consecrations.

5. Invocation of the deity.

"The gates of heaven were opened

The gates of earth were opened

The route of the sea was opened

The route of the rivers was opened

My spirit was heard by Gods and daimons

My spirit was heard by the spirit of heaven

My spirit was heard by the terrestrial spirit

My spirit was heard by the marine spirit

My spirit was heard by the riverine spirit

Therefore give spirit to the ring

I have prepared

O Gods whom I have named and called on

Give breath to the ring

Let its mouth be opened

so that it may breath and live

According to the Egyptian way -

Ei IEOU - Oh Hail

According to the Jews

Ei IEOU - Oh Hail

According to the Greeks
Ei IEOU - Oh Hail

According to the High Priests of Egypt
Ei IEOU - Oh Hail

According to the Hindus
Ei IEOU - Oh Hail

Consecrate and empower this object for me,
for the entire and glorious time of my life.

TO USE THE RING OR MAGICAL OBJECT:

There is a short, invocation that one can recite whenever one has need
of special power from the ring:

"The gates of heaven was opened
The gates of earth was opened
The route of the sea was opened
The route of rivers was opened
My spirit was heard by all Gods and daimons
My spirit was heard by the spirit of heaven
My spirit was heard by the terrestrial spirit
My spirit was heard by the marine spirit
My spirit was heard by the riverine spirit
Therefore give spirit to the mystery
I have prepared
O Gods whom I have named and have called on
Give breath to the mystery I have prepared.

Finish with a litany of 15 God's names. The traditional names are hopelessly garbled so I'd suggest either using your own or as I have, substituting those of the lunar days from the temple of Horus at Edfu:

EI IEOU Na (Oh Hail Red Serpent)
(pronounced Ai Ee-Ah-Ou with emphasis on the first syllable)

EI IEOU Shem (Oh Hail The stranger)

EI IEOU Irymeryef (Oh Hail The merry maker)

EI IEOU Wenet (Oh Hail The Hare Goddess)

EI IEOU Khnoum (Oh Hail)

EI IEOU Horus (Oh Hail his father's offspring)

EI IEOU Nehes (Oh Hail Goddess)

EI IEOU Thoth (Oh Hail)

EI IEOU Horus (Oh Hail avenger of his father)

EI IEOU Osiris (Oh Hail)

EI IEOU Amseti (Oh Hail)

EI IEOU Hapi (Oh Hail)

EI IEOU Tiamutef (Oh Hail)

EI IEOU Kebsenef (Oh Hail)

EI IEOU Iretef (Oh Hail)

HERMETICISM AND THE
PAGAN HERMENEUTIC OF MAGICK

The above spell has a complex structure that is characteristic of "grimoires" of this time in Roman Egypt and elsewhere. These principles have universal applicability. The spell has five parts:

1. An address to the triple Sun
2. Assumption of the God form
3. Hymn to the All Lord (Demiurge)
4. Hexametrical Hymn to the All Lord
5. Invocation of the deity.

The theoretical counterpart of this magick is a set of short dialogues (Libellos) known as the *Corpus Hermeticum*. The *Corpus Hermeticum* belongs to a Pagan world that felt itself under threat from the rise of a new, fanatical religion that came to be known as Christianity. Under this onslaught, classical Pagans developed a new sense of their own identity as Pagans, and rallied behind a manifesto known as Hermeticism. Hermeticism combined the best elements of Greek, Babylonian and above all Egyptian magical religion. Hermeticism is part of a *fightback* and resistance to the rising tide of fundamentalism. Fundamentalism and fanaticism are exclusive religious views of the kind "we are right and everyone else is wrong". Unlike Paganism, the Christians were militant and viewed anyone who did not sign up for their army of God as a civilian, literally a "Pagan".

The *Corpus Hermeticum* represents a crash course in the main tenets of the Pagan religious view. It is the ancient equivalent of a magical correspondence course. In it we read that the candidate enters a fellowship of *like-minded* individuals, of both sexes, who share a common aim. Initiates of *all* levels of attainment gather *together* to learn of the Hermetic way from experienced adepts.

The ultimate aim of Hermeticism is to raise oneself up through a series of steps to a final state of "gnosis" in which one becomes like a God. The Hermetic magicians shared a common view, plan or to use a technical term, a cosmology. This divine plan was a hierarchical vision of creation as divided into a series of steps ascending from the base to the top of the pyramid or symbolic mountain. Creation implied a creator who stands above a divine hierarchy and from whom its various parts emanate.

Egyptologists call this system the Heliopolitan theology. Heliopolis is the Greek name for the ancient city of "Iunu", just outside modern Cairo. It was centre of the all important Solar cult.

The Heliopolitan theology is one of the most famous aspects of the Egyptian magical religion. It describes a holy family of Gods - Ra, Geb, Nuit, Shu, Tefnut, Isis, Osiris, Seth & Nephthys. It is the family relationship between these Gods that is so revealing of Egyptian theology.

The founder of the family, known as the All-Lord or All-Father, is the God Ra. Sometime round 1350BCE during the Kingship of Ramesses II, Egypt experienced some big religious changes. Amongst them was the rise to prominence of a God known simply as *Amun*. Amun means 'hidden one' thus we can surmise that this God signifies some sort of *hidden* or mysterious power. Amun may originally have also been some sort of "lord of winds"- understood as the bodily breath but also the four winds, which are sometimes personified as four primary couples:

Amun   -   Amaunet;
Nun   -   Naunet;
Kek   -   Kauket;
Huh   -   Hauket. [66]

Amun is therefore quite a complex cosmic deity whose cult eventually fused with that of the Sun God Ra. Thus the *All-Lord* or *All-Father* is also known as Amun-Ra. Although in Egyptian religion as in later Hermeticism this All-Lord is bisexual meaning male *and* female.

This system is well-known because it has survived in many inscriptions. Ra or Amun-Ra is translated into the Greek system as *Helios* - the sungod. In the *Corpus Hermeticum* and related practical texts, the ultimate Creator and source of the cosmos is often referred to as Helios. The Creator is assisted in the task of emanating the cosmos by other divine forces, most notably Thoth. The ideas of the *Corpus Hermeticum*, written in Greek, are entirely compatible with the Egyptian magical religion!

This Egyptian theological scheme can be arranged into a hierarchical tree, reminiscent of many later mystical arrangements such as the Golden Dawn "Tree of Life".[67]

The whole schema looks thus

---

66. This is the "Ogdoad" - the theology of Hermopolis, cult centre of Thoth etc).
67. Hebrew: *Etz haChayim*; Greek: *Tetratis*

Amun-Ra (Solar Crown)

Shu (Wind)   +   Tefnut (Fire)

Geb (Earth)   +   Nuit (Sky)

Isis + Osiris;   Set(h) + Nephthys

These God names have their Greek equivalents. In the Ring Spell transcribed above I gave them in their original Egyptian form based on a Greek text which actually renders them:

Amun Ra	=	Helios
Shu	=	"Sender of Winds" (See *Decans* discussed later)
Tefnut	=	Aphrodite
Geb	=	Kronus
Nuit	=	Mother of the Gods
Osiris	=	Osiris
Isis	=	Isis
Seth	=	Typhon
Nephthys	=	Esenephus (A phonetic writting of Nephthys)

The spell mentions a secret *unspeakable* name and this is also in keeping with a literal reading of Amun meaning "mysterious". So the theology of the spell is quintessentially Egyptian. This is also the basic theology of Hermeticism.

The opening dialogues or "libellos" of the *Corpus Hermeticum* introduce the idea that our universe was created, and the Creator God is both male *and* female. This mysterious God stands at the beginning of a series of divine emanations of which we and our earthly plane, are the final and lowest level. It was once thought that Hermetic texts were essentially works of the Greek mind with Egyptian local colour. Actually they are "Pagan" texts in the truest sense, combining the best of Egyptian, Babylonian and Greek magical religion. Indeed later magick is also a synthesis or pan-religious phenomenon - incorporating elements from Judaism, Christianity and Islam.

The "Pagan" or "Hermetic" way has changed little since it was codified in Roman Egypt. Magick is still widely seen as a path to spiritual liberation. Magick is the "path of return" to the source. The magician rises, ascends or transcends through ever finer layers of existence. Magical spells are more often than not aids to this process of ascent. In the classical world this was called "theurgy" - literally the "work of God". This approach is very old and is certainly part of the older Egyptian magical religion. One can see this in for example the ancient Egyptian *Book of Gates* which is all about this mystical journey that ends when the magician flings open the doors of heaven or gates of earth (See my rendering of *The Book of Gates* below.)

In the ancient world, Egyptian priests were reknowned for their wisdom. The above shows there was real substance to this view. In fact when it came to special knowledge of the divine names, high priests were a class apart. If you look at the fifth part of the spell, the Gods are hailed and welcomed according to the Egyptian, Jewish and other ways. The "High Priests" of Egypt get an additional mention in their own right!

2. Assumption of the God form

The second part of the ring spell is all about the "assumption of the God form", something still widely used in modern magick. The interaction between these priests, and I'd say adepts of the Egyptian magical religion is very intimate. The *Corpus Hermeticum* adopts a similar point of view, the magician boldly stating: "*I am* etc etc." This progression from "I *summon* you, x" through various stages until the magician states : "I *am* x" - implies that one moves from duality to identification/assimilation with God. The devotee merges his or her consciousness with the Divine. There is no reason to think all Egyptian cults, even that of Seth, understand it as so.

It is also noteworthy that the spell implies that the divine body and physical nature are counterparts - to use the familiar terms of the Hermetica and other classical texts - they are connected as microcosm/macrocosm - "as above, so below".

3-5 Invocation & Devotion

Another crucially important thing that emerges from these rituals, especially with the invocation and hymn to the Sun-God, is the devotional side of magick. This gives the lie to all those commentators who suggest that magick is a purely technocratic pursuit.

5. The spell also provides us with an important example of the "vowel" magick described earlier. The magician recites a litany of 15 Godnames. The 15 recitations of the formulae may be *lunar* in intent - one for each day of the lunar half month. Each name is prefaced with the call "EI IEOU" - vocalised as "Ay IAOU". Is this pure vowel song - probably? Although some recent research suggests that in Egyptian this had an actual meaning - 'Oh Hail' (ʿI i3w).

This ancient ritual to first consecrate and then use a magical ring of power is based upon Egyptian religious ideas and techniques. In fact the original title of the spell, written in Demotic, likens it to the very old Egyptian litany of "opening the mouth". This ceremony formed part of the mummification process but was also applied to the animation of cult objects such as statues, buildings and in this instance a magical ring.

A long time ago I learnt that wearing a special ring or talisman is a good way to keep one's magical quest in mind during the hussle and bustle of mundane life.

COLOUR SYMBOLISM

The primary colours are:
Red Ochre = Fire / Blood
Yellow Ochre = Eternity / Gold
Copper Blue = Sky & Waters
Malachite Green = Living things
Carbon Black = Night, death and Osirian otherworld
Chalk White = Purity

To state the obvious, ancient Egypt was a very visual culture. Symbols abound and what we moderns call symbolism is still an important way of interpreting the underlying meaning of many things. Although not obvious from presentation in books, every hieroglyph, is coloured in a natural or logical way, ie red for the Sun and yellow for the Moon; the same darker tones used for men, and women respectively. Parts of the body are red, vegetation is green although some have a symbolic colour – hence bread is blue and metal sometimes red rather than black. Hair is black or blue. The Goddess Nephthys is blue, as often is the Ankh rather than the yellow one might expect for fabric. So colour correspondences are mutable, mostly for stylistic reason but also perhaps because of some principles we no longer fully understand. Thus the "knot of Isis" should be fabric yellow but is often shown as red or its *contrary* colour - green. Precious and semi-precious stones were utilised more for the colour opportunities they presented rather than other intrinsic qualities. [67]

NUMBER

1

Oneness – individuality & permanence. But often unstable as monads have an inherent capacity to create.

2

Duality & Unity. The God "Heruifi" in the *Book of Gates* has two heads, one of Horus and one of Set, which perhaps implies an underlying unity behind the duality. "Eternity" has two aspects – male (neheh) and female (djet).

3

Plurality – witness the ubiquitous hieroglyph of three strokes used to represent great number. See also the rare triple headed image of "Ash"

---

67. For this section the following books were useful: Malek, Jaromir (2000) *Egyptian Art*, Phaidon; Wilkinson, R H (1992) *Reading Egyptian Art*, T&H, Wilkinson, R H (1994) *Symbol & Magic in Egyptian Art* T&H; Schafer, H (translated by J Baines 1971) *Principles of Egyptian Art*.

which may represent plurality or the cyclical nature of a thing. Egyptian liturgy is often repeated three times.

4

Totality and completeness - see for example the fourfold Djed pillar and also the four baboons often shown on the base of obelisks etc. Heaven is also envisioned as a four-sided canopy (see for example the heaven hieroglyph) but viewed from one edge or side so that one only sees the supporting poles nearest – hence two by extension here represents four.

5

Other numbers meaning is derived from principal four:

6

2 x 3

7

4 + 3 i.e. plurality and completeness

42 judges = 6 x 7

8

2 x 4 i.e. totality doubled

9

3 x 3 i.e. plurality trebled viz: a great number

10

Space & time. Ten days in a week but also a ten-day period or decan is a basic unit of measurement in astronomical charts.

12

The Egyptians were the first to divide the day into 12 parts or hours, although length of these hours would vary according to time of year.

THE EGYPTIAN "ALPHABET", "KABBALAH" NUMBER, MEANINGS

"What Ptah has created and Thoth has written down"[68]

The God Ptah as patron of artists etc, crafted the hieroglyphic signs, as the shapes and names of everything. Thoth's role is to make the script that embodies the sounds of what was already there.[69]

Because the world is so complex Ptah had to make more than 800 signs in order to fully describe everything. But underlying this is a basic structure of just 24 *phonemes* or alphabetic signs with which we can vocalise the name of all things in our world.

As time went by the number of phonemes expanded. Egyptian, like many ancient languages did not express vowels in the written script. This does not mean there were no vowels merely that their written form was kept as a scribal secret. The vowels can be considered as the hidden heart or "soul" of the language.

In the period when Egyptians were ruled by Greeks, the people spoke a less formal, vernacular form of Egyptian for which the Greeks coined the term "Demotic" meaning "popular". Egyptian Demotic was written in 28 signs. It is as well to remind yourself that the Greeks considered

---

68. Continues: "the heaven with its constellations/the Earth and what it contains,/what the mountain spew out,/what the inundation moistens, what the Sun illuminates,/and what grows upon the back of the Earth" Onomasticon of Amenemope from Alan H Gardner, *Ancient Egyptian Onomastica* (Word Lists) , 3 vols, Oxford Clarendon Press 1947 vol 1 *1.
69. Jan Assmann *Moses the Egyptian* (Harvard 1997 : 115).

the lunar month to have approximately 28 days, as did many of the cultures that came after the Egyptian such as the Arab.

The Romans took over Egypt from the Greeks. This last period coincides with the final stage of the native language when it is becomes Coptic. The underlying language doesn't change but it is written in a mix of Greek and Demotic characters. The motivation for this change is probably the desire by Coptic Christians to dispense entirely with the "Pagan" hieroglyphs, whilst at the same time expanding the total number of characters to 30. [70]

Again remind yourself that the Egyptians considered the lunar month to have 30 days.

In order to understand and use Egyptian magick from this time, there is no need to fully understand the Egyptian language. Indeed the system now transcended any particular language and became international and universal. Nevertheless it is necessary to be aware of some of the basic building blocks derived from the original alphabet.

As I mentioned, there is a rough equivalence between the characters of the alphabet and the days of the lunar month. With the rise of Arab sorcery this relationship between the (Arabic) alphabet and the lunar days was maintained. It is from this stream of thought that a great deal of modern magick draws its inspiration and techniques. Aleph is the first letter in all these languages - Egyptian, Greek, Hebrew or Arabic. Aleph corresponds with or is the alphabet's *New Moon*. For me this is

---

70. Twenty-five Greek characters and six retained Egyptian Demotic.

new and incomplete knowledge. But some things are certain. The following table shows the entire list of available Egyptian phonemes and a hypothetical correspondence to the lunar cycle:

Lunar Day	Sign	Transliteration	Sound	Image	Numerology	Hieroglyph
1	ꜣ	Aleph		Vulture	1	
2	ỉ	Yodh		Flowering reed	2	
3	y	y		Two reed flowers	3	
4	ꜥ	'ain		forearm	4	
5	w			quail chick	5	
6	b			foot	6	
7	p			stool	7	
8	f			horned viper	8	
9	m			owl	9	
10	n			water	10	
11	r			mouth	100	
12	h			Reed shelter	200	
13	ḥ	emphatic h		wick of twisted flax	300	
14	ḫ	ch as in loch		placenta	400	
15	ẖ	ch as in German	animal's belly with teats	500	
16	s			bolt	600	
17	š			pool	700	
18	ḳ	qoph		hill slope	800	
19	k	kaph		basket with handle	900	
20	g	hard g		stand for jar	1000	
21	t			loaf	2000	
22	ṯ	tj		tow rope	3000	
23	d			hand	4000	
24	ḏ	dj		snake	5000	
25	Epsilon				6000	
26	Eta				7000	
27	Iota				8000	
28	Omicron				9000	
29	Upsilon				10000	
30	Omega				100000	

Take 24 Characters of Middle Egyptian and add six Greek vowels to the end. (Coptic added six extra

Ways to use this table

In my magical group, our rituals have acquired a spirit-house cum lunar clock. We added an image of the Vulture, (Egyptian hieroglyph Aleph) for the Zero Hour or 12 o'clock. Next is the Horned Viper (F) at 3 o'clock and Moon's First Quarter; 6 o'clock is the Owl and the Phallic Bolt (Seth) is at 9 o'clock.

THE SODALITY OF THE MAGI

You may be wondering whether ancient magicians ever banded together in groups much as do modern practitioners? Some modern commentators have argued that the magicians of this time were solitary practitioner perhaps even "lonely". [71]

Fritz Graf is a great scholar and few would wish to disagree with his analysis. For me it shows that both kinds of practitioner existed. The solitary, hierarchical focused mage, who is as familiar to us now as he or she was no doubt 2000 years ago. But are we failing to see the wood for the trees? The Theban magical library is the complete collection of one family of adepts. Its context has to be viewed in the round. In my opinion it should be read in conjunction with the *Corpus Hermeticum*, which is

---

71. Fritz Graf in "The Magician's Initiation." *Helios* 21.2. (1994). 161-77: says: "p. 166. There are traces of social bonds between magicians. Both cooperation and a feeling of community existed among practitioners – at least, they could call a colleague "fellow mystes" and refer to a more advanced practitioner as a "mystagogos". Moreover, some stories suggest it was better to learn the craft from experts, especially from Egyptian priests, which implies interaction with colleagues. In this respect, however, the **papyri themselves tell a different story**. Although some spells pretend to have been transmitted from a father to his son or daughter, or from a mighty magician to a king, and

the *theosophical* counterpart to the operational magick. The same group of people participate in both. The *Corpus Hermeticum* reveals a definite sense of community, peer groups and even collective rites. My own reading of current research shows that magicians sprung from many social classes, were of both genders, were often social, inter-married and lived in groups. [72]

HERMENEIA

Our study of ancient Egypt learns much from preliterate, prehistoric sources. We can cast our minds way back into the mist when our spiritual nature began to stir, perhaps as a shamanic frenzy or moment of quiet liturgy beside the corpse of a departed family member.

---

although the letter is among the literary forms used for magical instruction, overall, the papyri portray the magician as a lonely individual who will use the texts for his own initiation and for the different practices prescribed; the advice to use a mystagogue for part of some of the rituals or the possibility of working together with a colleague are rare exceptions to this rule. Moreover, even when colleagues cooperated, distrust was always present: one of the few texts that use the term "synmystes" – the Mithras Liturgy – makes it clear that different degrees of involvement in the rite should be retained. When the magician performed the rite with a colleague, the latter had to follow the same rules of purity as the magician himself; given the dangers inherent in the praxis, this is only logical. But even when the colleague fulfilled all such requirements (p.167) he was not made privy to the magician's secrets: the spell instructed the magician to speak some essential prayers softly enough that his colleague could not hear them (lines 744-5). In ritual as in ideology, hierarchy, rather than community was the aim of the magician."

72. See Garth Fowden (1996) *The Egyptian Hermes*, Cambridge

The Egyptians had secrets. One that they were most anxious to forget comes from that time. This is before the emergence of the state, unified and ruled by the famous Pharaohs or kings. The Egyptians went to great lengths to eraze the memory of what came before. Forgotten were the ancient Pagan tribes, the proto city-states such as legendary Nagada (citadel of Seth) and Hierakonpolis (City of the Hawk), all were forgotten and replaced with other myths such as "The unification of Egypt" or "divine kingship".

Egyptian culture was already old when they began to record their journey. We join them beside the sarcophagus of a dead chieftain. Together with the new king we can peek at the corpse of a deceased father or mother. Or we could cast our minds back to the very remote past, to the very beginnings of this rite.

Over the petrified corpse, the favoured child, witnessed, indeed performed a ceremony later known as the "Opening of the Mouth". Then he or she slept, waiting for the visitation of the departed in a dream. When the vision comes the magick work was done and the living could move on.

Egypt's famous "mummies" are fetish objects. That is to say they are 'made by art'. We may not be able to match the Egyptians in the beauty of his or her mummy but we can still *animate* an object with magical power or cause a spirit to dwell there.

In our new age we use the more neutral word *statue* for these same fetish objects. The long process of mummification so familiar to us from the high culture of ancient Egypt is very like the creation of a statue. The once living flesh is, over the course of 72 days and nights, turned to stone. The Egyptians called this rite 'Ouphor' - the Ceremony of Opening the Mouth.

Some say that texts such as those found on the walls of the pyramids are actually "describing experiences of the living not the dead." [73]

Despite what the expert Egyptologists may say, most 'amateurs' have for some time been convinced that ancient pyramids were never intended as tombs but had some additional, perhaps even central purpose in an Egyptian 'mystery' or 'initiatory cult'. This belief is bolstered by a succession of books on the 'mysteries' of the pyramids that seize upon the fact that many, if not most Egyptian tombs are empty. Ah, say the Egyptologists, that's because kings often did have more than one tomb.[74]

The term 'shamanism' has been used to spare the blushes of those who find magick embarrassing. Shamanism is a very interesting concept that does have some relevance to Egyptian religion, especially for pre-dynastic times. But I'd say 'magical' wisdom is as accurate and indeed may be closer to the Egyptian activity. It is as well to recall that they had no equivalent for our word *religion*, whereas they did constantly use the term *Heka*, the deployment of divine power, a technique later translated by the Roman word magic.

Whether you call the Egyptian high culture 'shamanic' or as I prefer 'magical', its *written* story begins with the so-called Pyramid texts.

---

73. Naydler (2005: 311)
74. For example Queen Hatshepsut, whose ambitions grew after she became co-regent with her stepson Thutmose III – so much so that she had need from something grander than her already completed tomb of earlier times, when she was King's chief wife. Forbes 2005 in KMT Vol 16 No 3)

Perhaps the first problem when decoding the pyramids is to decide in what order to read these texts? Does the narrative begin at the front entrance and work inwards to the sarcophagus chamber? Or does it begin at the sarcophagus chamber and continue outwards to the front door. You can surely see the importance of knowing how the transiting 'shaman' or if you follow the conventional interpretation, the deceased, was meant to 'read' the *signposts* in the pyramid or tomb. [75]

The current academic theory is that two interlocking narratives begin in the innermost sarcophagus chamber with two sequences of ritual. The first is a complex offering ritual to the deceased. The second is a 'resurrection' rite or 'soul journey'. There are also two distinct actors in the rites, the priest performing the complex offerings or chants, and the deceased king, whose spirit (*Akh*) is 'reanimated' by the ritual and thereafter begins its 'ghostly' journey out of the pyramid.

The *Akh* is one of three most tangible aspects of a living being – the other two being the *Ka* and the *Ba*. The *Akh* is represented in hieroglyphic by the crested Ibis (*Geronticus eremita*). Recent research suggests that *Akh* as a sound represents the call of this bird.

---

75. The great scholar Alexandre Piankoff tells us that the pyramid of Unas is a landmark in the history of ancient Egypt. It is the earliest pyramid having inscriptions in its interior, thus making it one of the oldest literary monuments of Egypt! Unas, the last king (or Pharaoh if you like) of the 5th Dynasty, reigned over Egypt about 2375-2345 BC. His pyramid was called "Perfect Are the Places of Unas."
Alexandre Piankoff (1954-1974) *Egyptian Religious Texts and Representations*, 6 vols (vol 5 1968 for Pyramid of Unas), Bollingen
76. G25 in the signlist

The Akh (not to be confused with Ankh) is the *spiritualised* or transfigured body that in the pyramid texts goes to heaven. Abandoning the mummified corpse, the disembodied spirit retraces the path through the corridors and antechambers until it opens the doors of heaven and is then ferried into the night sky by the God Seth. There, the deceased King's spirit (Akh or astral body) joins the imperishable northern stars.

Is Egyptian religion really obsessed with the needs of the 'dead'? Is there a 'mystery' or contemplative element wherein the aim is some form of liberation for the living? A close examination of the 'mechanics' of Egyptian magick reveals how the dead are in fact *beneficial for* the living.

Some say the pyramid texts were not exclusively funeral texts; they were also 'transfiguration texts' that had to be memorised by those 'kingly shamans'. In this view, the soul's journey is also accomplished by the king on our behalf. The king acts as vicarious shaman for the whole of Egypt. Was he, as some say, whilst living, sealed in a sarcophagus and then left alone to make his 'shamanic' journey out of the pyramid. Does that sound likely?

Or is the soul's journey some form of 'out of the body experience' (OBE). Now I'm not denying there are hundreds of interesting accounts of OBEs in the literature. But these all seem to be spontaneous, accidental happenings often triggered by unrepeatable, traumatic events such as being violently struck on the head! But occultism requires a more reliable, less dangerous approach – does it not?

Neuro-Linguistic Programming (NLP) reveals differences between people in terms of their ability to associate or dissociate from an experience. One person will tend to completely disassociate from their body during trance (the old OBE) model whilst others, probably the majority, will always retain some connection with their body. The point being that whether one is associated or disassociated, the results, in terms of mystical knowledge (what the ancients called 'Gnosis') is much the same. Stop worrying about OBEs and you can still explore the astral otherworld, albeit in a less dramatic way.

I suspect that the restricted spaces of the pyramids and tombs wouldn't lend themselves to this kind of activity. For example the festival hall used in life to celebrate the king's jubilee or Heb Sed, is in many pyramid complexes (cities of the dead) merely a dummy building or façade. The offering chamber in front of the tomb is a different matter entirely and was obviously designed to be visited by the living and as a *theatre* for communication with the dead.

The traces of 'shamanic wisdom' in the pyramids texts do not, in my opinion, belong to Pharaonic times at all, which was much more focussed on the *spacial* relationships, in older terminology geomancy or what we might these days call mind maps. The traces of shamanism there belong to an earlier age, that of the late Neolithic, when a non-literate red land culture prospered at Ombos before the coming of the Horus kings! Thus one of the final acts of the transfigured Pharaoh always remained to call upon the ancient red ochre God Seth, to remove his finger (phallus?) from the eye or body of Horus, to thereby open the gates and ferry one over to the imperishable stars which he, Seth, then leads in their diurnal circumambulation of the northern sky.

In truth there is another less well-known magical tradition of ancient Egypt. This is the folk tradition which underlies much of this material. The folk tradition is like an ancient river. Its origins lie far away - but it is deep and wide and still flowing.

ARE THE GODS OUR FRIENDS?

Whatever the Egyptians may have thought about their Gods, there are many clear instances when they were also unwanted entities that needed to be banished. One of many famous examples of this is the so-called anti-Osirienne incantation found in the consecration ritual of the pyramid of Pepi I : [77]

[...]

§1267 Let not Osiris come in this his evil coming,
do not open to him thine arms.
Away, run to Nedit! Quick, run to Adja!

§1268 Let not Horus come in this his evil coming,
do not open to him thine arms.

---

77. Piankoff (1968 :7)

Hurry to Mendes! Away, hurry to Isieion!

§1269 Let not Seth come in this his evil coming,
do not open to him thine arms.
Remember that he was called CASTRATED ONE.

You get the picture. The folk knew that gods can sometimes be troublesome.

ARE THE GODS EVIL?

Contemporary magical practitioners have always been interested in the 'problem of evil' - the nature of good and bad action. Take for example Helena Blavatsky's statement - 'demon est deus inversus'.[79] This was later adopted by the poet W B Yeats as his magical motto in the Order of the Golden Dawn.

Most practitioners believe that the ancient Egyptian God Seth is the prototype for the contemporary archetype of Lucifer, Satan or the Devil. But in truth, all Egyptian Gods, perhaps all Gods have good and bad sides.

The great Egyptologist Erik Hornung wrote: "The Gods of Egypt can be terrifying, dangerous and unpredictable, but they cannot be evil. Originally this was true even of Seth, the murderer of Osiris. Battle, constant confrontation, confusion and questioning of the established order, in all of which Seth engages as a sort of "trickster", are all necessary

---

78. An avatar of Seth
79. See her highly influential and monumental work *The Secret Doctrine* (1888:1.411).

features of the existent world and of the limited disorder that is essential to a living order. But Gods and people must together ensure that disorder does not come to overpower justice and order and this is the meaning of their common obligation toward Ma'at." [80]

EGYPTIAN MAGICK AND HERMETICISM?

'The Gods rejoice when invoked according to the rites
of the Egyptians'
- Iamblicus, *On the Mysteries of Egypt* [81]

"Hermeticism is a set of philosophical and religious beliefs based primarily upon the writings attributed to Hermes Trismegistus, ...a wise sage and Egyptian priest, and who is commonly seen as synonymous with the Egyptian God Thoth. These beliefs are central to the Western magical traditions. The Hermetic cult even gets a mention in the *Koran* as the Sabians " (Wikipedia)

The Greek sounding name "Hermes Trismegistos" was designed to cast a veneer over an Egyptian matrix. In a nutshell the Greek rulers of Egypt appropriated the magical wisdom of ancient Egypt whilst at the same time operating a system of cultural apartheid that eventually led to its complete suppression. [82]

---

80. Erik Hornung, *Conceptions of God in ancient Egypt : the one and the many*, translated by J Baines, (Cornell 1996); also Morgan 2011 "The Heart of Thelema: Morality, Amorality & Immorality in Aleister Crowley's Thelemic cult" Pomegranate Vol 13 no 2
81. VII 5 257-258
82. Dieleman (2005 : 106) for division between use of Greek & Egyptian languages.

Until quite recently most scholarly commentators would say Egyptian wisdom is an oxymoron. Consequently the eminent Egyptologist Sir Alan Gardiner, recalls that when Herodotus toured Egypt shortly after 450BCE., "he thought claims that 5th century philosophers like Thales and Pythagoras derived much of their wisdom from Egypt were *undoubtedly fictitious.*" He also warned his readers to be sceptical about similar claims made for Democritus and Plato.[84]

Standing as we do on the cusp of the new 21st century, all these issues are subject to widespread reappraisal. Eminent academic authorities such as Jan Assmann have challenged many old assumptions and transformed the way people see the Egyptian past:

> "[T]he basic concepts of the Hermetic doctrines are in fact deeply rooted in ancient Egyptian religious thought, which was still alive among Egyptian priests in the Roman period."[85]

Until recently there were very few textual sources for the Hermetic tradition; the principal one being the so-called *Corpus Hermeticum* - a collection of short, late-Egyptian treatises, contemporary with early Christianity.

One of the important principles of the *Corpus Hermetica* concerns the cosmic significance of sound and vibration. Treatise XVI purports to be a letter, written in Greek by Asclepius, a student of Hermes Trismegistus, to King Ammon. The strange thing about this letter is that it begins with

---

84. Sir Alan Gardiner (1961) *Egypt of the Pharaohs*, OUP : 9
85. Dieleman (2005 : 2)

an explanation that the Hermetic mysteries only really make sense in the Egyptian tongue! This is taken to mean that "The very quality of the sound and the (intonation) of the Egyptian words contain in themselves the energy of the objects they speak of." [86] It is the sound that matters, the language or the handwriting is incidental.

Like many of the so-called Hermetic axioms it reminds me of the ancient Hindu world view, which lionises the creative power of sound. Esoteric Hinduism can be seen as a synthesis of the Egyptian power of the word with the *Orphic* power of sound. Hence the later Hindu culture famously makes great use of special sound patterns called "mantras" to *manipulate* reality. It is one of many parallels between the Egyptian magical religion and esoteric Hinduism.

The Egyptian priests were pragmatists. At the end of Egyptian history, in Roman Egypt, during the rise of Christianity, times were hard. The Romans had removed the traditional livelihood of the Egyptian priestly intellectual. This was the culmination of a long period of colonial exploitation, by the Persians, then the Greeks and finally the Romans.

To make ends meet "Egyptian priests played on the expectations of their customers, taking on the role of the exotic specialist..." [87] A game familiar to the modern practitioner who often finds it easier to live up to the expectations of the uninitiated.

---

86. Dieleman (2005 : 3)
87. Dieleman (2005 : 9)

As colonial subjects you'd expect they would reject the magical ideas of the Greeks. But this didn't happen. In fact many interesting aspects of Greek magick were combined with the Egyptian original. This is the origin of the so-called *Greek Magical Papyri* - also known as the *Theban Magical Library*. In truth the spells of the Theban Magican Library are multicultural and multilingual – "the result of a desire to collect and combine ritual texts of different origins." [88]

We know that the language of magick and medicine is international. Much of its terminology comes from the Egyptian temple.[89] Not surprisingly Egyptians often had a Greek personal name for public use and a native one for private.

HERMETIC PRAYER & RUBRIK

"As they left the sanctuary, they began praying to God and, turning to the south [90] (for when someone wants to entreat God at sunset, he should direct his gaze to that quarter, and likewise at sunrise toward the direction they call east) and they were already saying their prayer when in a hushed voice Asclepius asked : 'Tat, do you think we should suggest that your father tell them to add frankincense and spices as we pray to God?"

When Trismegistus heard him, he was disturbed and said "a bad omen, Asclepius, very bad. To burn incense and such stuff when you entreat God smacks of sacrilege.

---

88. Dieleman (2005 : 11)
89. Dieleman (2005 : 80)
90. The Sun at winter solstice sets at its most southerly point.

For he wants nothing who is himself all things and in whom all things are. Rather let us worship him by giving thanks [a voice offering], for Gods find mortal gratitude to be the best incense.

"We thank you, supreme and most high God, by whose grace along we have attained the light of your knowledge; holy name that must be honoured, the one name by which our ancestral faith blesses God alone, we thank you who deign to grant to all a father's fidelity, reverence and love, along with any power that is sweeter, by giving us the gift of consciousness, reason and understanding:
Consciousness, by which we may know you;
reason, by which we may seek you in our dim suppositions;
knowledge, by which we may rejoice in knowing you.

And we who are saved by your power do indeed rejoice because you have shown yourself to us wholly. We rejoice that you have deigned to make us Gods for eternity even while we depend on the body. For this is mankind's only means of giving thanks: knowledge of your majesty.

We have known you, the vast light reserved only by reason. We have understood you, true life of life, the womb pregnant with all coming-to-be. We have known you, who persists eternally by conceiving all coming-to-be in its perfect fullness.

Worshipping with this entire prayer the good of your goodness, we ask only this, that you wish us to persist in the love of your knowledge and that we never be cut off from such a life as this.

With such hopes we turn to a pure meal that includes no living thing."[91]

THE EGYPTIAN MAGICAL RELIGION

No systematic book of Egyptian theology has ever been found. One has to rely on inference and so-called "implicit" theology to reconstruct core beliefs and see how much they resemble our own. The modern discipline of Egyptology developed out of the European occult tradition and speculations about the lost mysteries of Egypt. So-called "scientific Egyptology" began as a reaction to the occult approach and therefore focussed more on technical linguistics rather than religious speculation. As a result many Egyptian "occult" texts endured a twilight existence, sidelined as "pure witchcraft". Thus you may well have heard of *The Book of the Dead* and *Pyramid texts* but not the *Books of the Underworld?* I have often used them as the basis of much of my own "Egyptian Liturgy".

---

91. Asclepius v 41 - trans Copenhaver 1992 : 92 see also CH XIII vs 16 where the instruction is to the South Wind. See NF (Nock & Festugière II 389 nn 341-2. cites other example including PGM V 422 "Sunrise and Moonrise" (Betz p 109; FR IV 244-5; Scott III 280, Braun, Jean pp 262-3.) - There is a closely related prayer PGM III 591-609 (494-591 spells omited)

There is also many neglected "folk magick" aspect of Egyptian magical religion whose importance is difficult to exagerate. [92]

Egyptian religion is sometimes defined as 'Realising Maat'. Maat, the principle of truth, justice and cosmic harmony was personified as a Goddess. But this is the big picture, religion considered in a wider sense. Jan Assmann suggests we could also consider Egyptian religion in another but equally important sense concerned with one's personal contact with the Gods and individual piety.

The Pagan theologian Iamblicus, wrote that religion in ancient Egypt was focused on two things:

1. The cult of the sun, and the continuation of the Sun's course
2. Protecting the mysteries of Abydos
   – the cult shrine of the God Osiris.

Solar mythology is therefore pretty central and our world is viewed as the unfolding (Kheperu) or emanation of the Sun God. The 19th dynasty of Ramesses and Sety circa 1350BCE is of particular significance in the development of this theology. The king's names were often written with the Kheper or Kheperu component.

---

92. See Jon Ray (2001) reflections of Osiris: Lines from Ancient Egypt, London Chapter 8 "The Dreams of the Twins in (Pap) St Petersburg" reprinted in Kasia Szpakowska (2006) *Through a Glass Darkly: Magic, dreams and prophesy in Ancient Egypt* (Swansea) pp 189-204.(See Iamblicus *De mysteriis VI*, 7, 282, see discussion of this in Assmann, Lecture at the Ritual Dynamics and the Science of Ritual Conference, Heidelberg Sept-Oct 2008)) (Jan Assmann (2001) *The Search for God in Ancient Egypt*, translated by David Lorton, Cornell)

A third more heterodox aspect to Egyptian religion is folk orientated and to do with the cult of the ancestors. We might call this the "left eye of Ra" - ie the realm of the moon, which is a secret key.

In the ancient world the Egyptians were considered to be very pious. We have already discussed the *Corpus Hermeticum* and its reference to Egypt as "the temple of the world". Modern Egyptians still love this explanation of the popularity of their country. Whereas in surrounding countries, the Gods, having completed their earthly tasks, were said to have withdrawn from the earth to the sky. For example in Israel, the priests "handed back" the keys of the Solomonic temple to angelic guardians before its destruction by the Babylonians.[93]

In Egypt this process was delayed, in part because of the ancient and continued maintenance of religious activity. These activities come in three kinds: [94]

1. Cultic – local or civil manifestation.
2. Mythic – i.e. stories of the Gods, often fabulous
3. Cosmic – divine action of Gods as in the myth of extra (epagomenal) days on the year.

---

93. B. Ta'anit 29a-b Our rabbis have taught: When the first temple was about to be destroyed bands upon bands of young priests with the key of the temple in their hands assembled and mounted the roof of the temple and exclaimed, 'Master of the Universe, as we did not have the merit to be faithful treasurer these keys are handed back into thy keeping'. They then threw the keys up towards heaven. And there emerged the figure of a hand and received the keys from them." (fn Tisha b'Av: An Historical Approach http://www.wlcj.org/upimages/ An_Historical_Approach.pdf)
94. Following Assmann (2001: 8)

1. Local or cultic dimensions

The 'concept of the city deity was one of the most ancient elements of Egyptian religion." [95] Egyptian cities seems to have developed out of primary mounds, perhaps the remnants of ancient tribal gathering places. Due to peculiaritues of Egyptian geology, the well known annual Nile flood actually resolves itself into forty-two enormous "temporary" lakes. The primevel first settlements began with the raised mounds of unflooded ground as their focal point. This is also the basis of the provinces known by the Greek term "nomes" (Egyptian : *sepat*).

Such places must have presented themselves as the natural choice for a temple. Mythology and geography are then unified in the form of a building. The ground plan of all temples is derived from the first primeval temple.[96] Temples are very special buildings, to borrow a term from Giordano Bruno, they are "Theatres of Memory".

In later times the Egyptians sought to preserve the *atmosphere* of the first temple. Thus the Ptolemaic (Greek) temple of Horus at Edfu adheres very closely to an ancient paradigm. It was built towards the end of Egyptian history when the ideas were under threat. The architects went to enormous lengths to reify the core elements of Egyptian culture in this design.

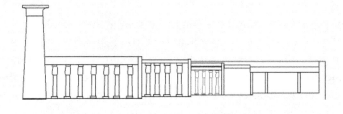

---

95.   Assmann (2001 : 27)
96.   Assmann (2001 : 30)

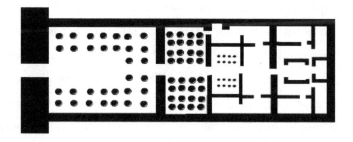

Whereas secular dwellings were largely constructed in mudbrick, sacred architecture enjoyed a virtual monopoly on the use of stone. The ancient cityscape was based around this very visible dichotomy.

The temple is an "image of the celestial horizon" (*akhet*) - the sky above, earth, with plants growing upwards.[97] The temple either settles the Gods in the land or cuts out a piece for them to possess. The God within is a universal God – a conception that makes its first appearance during the time of the Ramesside kings, whose family affiliations were actually to the God Seth. The distinctive eastern façade of the temple looks like the notch on the eastern horizon, the "doors of heaven" from whence the Sun God makes his first appearance at dawn.

---

97. Assmann (2001: 37)

Thus the temple is an image of the cosmos. And Egypt is "the temple of the world". Right from the very beginning a temple records and teaches us details about its mythological origin. This can be via actual texts such as those carved on the walls at Edfu. Or more esoterically as in the "secrets" memorialized in the shape of the building. This tradition continues through time and can be seen in the design of medieval cathedrals and churches.

Which raises the question of the origin of religious experience? Is it, as some say, in those cult acts beside the grave of a loved one? Or do its roots lie in something even more mystical, even shamanic? The extreme antiquity of temples and shrines suggests that from the very beginning religious activity was collective. Some will even argue, as does Jan Assmann, that collective experience came chronologically prior to the individual variety. People made special artefacts found in even the simplest grave or tomb. These objects are then given life or a soul, a "Ba" by the Gods, becoming a permanent part of the tribal memory.

One of the most archaic of such rites comes down to us as "The Ceremony of Opening the Mouth". This ritual still forms the secret basis of some modern magick. In times of yore, the principal actor in this archaic funeral rite were the surviving children or heirs. To secure an inheritance one was required to sleep by the deceased, awaiting a vision in a dream. As we saw earlier in connection with the Ring spell, the same rite was used on statues, amulets and rings. So the final act in the consecration of an object would be confirmation via a dream. [98]

---

98. Assmann (2001 : 45)

It is a moot point as to what or who was the original subject of the ritual. Was it something done for the dead and then later extended to other "inanimate" objects? Or did it perhaps begin as an act bringing a magical object or fetish to life? The ceremony of opening the mouth was also performed as a temple dedication. This rite is the "finishing touch" to any cult object, the moment the spirit or "Ba" of the particular God is encouraged to take up residence.

Magick continues to use some of these techniques either in name or deed. Sometimes the mere calling to mind of the name of the rite (eg "Ouphor") is enough to invoke its power (*baraka*).

The power to *animate* or *entice* a spirit into a statue is also described in the *Corpus Hermetica*.[99] This technique was one the early Christian theoreticians found particularly repellant. The passage on making statues may even have been deleted from selections of *Corpus Hermetica* used in Christian communities. The second of the ten commandments specifically forbids the making of idols. Herein lies the origin of the widespread Abrahamic taboo and indeed fear of this kind of magick.

THE COSMOS

Hermeticism is a late classical development of Egyptian magical-religion. The "late classical" period is more or less synonymous with the period of the Roman empire, the classical world's "last gasp" if you will. Despite what you might think, this is actually an interesting, creative and dynamic time for the Egyptian magical culture.

---

99. "Asclepius" vs 24sq in Copenhaver (1995: 81sq)

The Hermetic magician Iamblicus tells us that the Egyptians could be very naturalistic in their view of the world. From earliest times the Gods were seen as guardians and ruled by natural laws. They tended to focus on natural forces and things of immediate concern. The Egyptian love of "astrology" and stellar lore is a good example of this crossover between the natural and the supernatural. Although the validity of astrology is often disputed in the modern world, it is an important example of the interplay between the mundane and the divine world, where deities are themselves subject to natural laws. To illustrate this consider the mythology of the Egyptian Goddess Nuit.

THE STAR GODDESS

Aleister Crowley's evocation of Nuit (or Newet) in *Liber AL* [100] focuses our attention on a very unusual and unique Egyptian Goddess. The sky Goddess Nuit is one of the oldest deities in the Egyptian pantheon. Her first appearance in prehistory was as a clan deity. The really old Goddesses **often had bovine form. Thus Nuit is described in** *Pyramid Text* spell 548 as a long horned celestial cow who suckles the king and takes him to herself in the sky: "May Nuit the Great put her hands on him/ she the long of horn, the pendulous of breast". Over time she assume human form.

---

100. Notes for short presentation at Treadwell's, April 9th 2012. Feast for the reception of the *Book of the Law*, organised by Entelechy, Greece. Main sources consulted Morgan, M, *Wheel of the Year in Ancient Egypt* (Mandrake) for transcription of the "Book of Nuit" ritual drama, linked to one of thirteen lunar feasts of the archaic ritual year. Hollis, Susan T "Women of Ancient Egypt and the sky Goddess Nut" *Journal of American Folklore* 100 (1987). Hollis, Susan T "Five Egyptian Goddesses in the third millennium BC" KMT 5,4 (1994) 48-49; Lesko, Barbara (1999) S *The Great Goddesses of Egypt*;

In many mythologies the sky is a God, i.e. male and its counterpart is the Great Earth Mother. The Egyptian personification of the sky as female is unique.

Her name literally means "The watery one" (Nw.t). She represents "the sky" but not as a lifeless roof of heaven but as a dynamic entity, creating and destroying. She also represented the entire sky, night and day as well as large features such as the Milky Way. [101]

All the above reflects the high status of women in ancient Egypt. She is "the reassuring image of the Great Mother to whom we all return at death, the holy mother who can resurrect the dead, the sacred womb from which the dead are reborn". These truths endured from very earliest times right until the end of historic Egypt. [102]

The Egyptian *Pyramid Texts*, possibly some of the world's oldest religious literature, contain spells asking her to conceal Osiris from Seth, to take possession of the earth and to install every God who has a bark as an imperishable star in the starry sky – that is in Nuit herself. [103]

Who created her? Originally she was the daughter of the first primary couple, Shu & Tefnut meaning air and fire. These are quite amorphous deities. In later myths she is married to Geb, the personification of the Earth. Some say the story of her separation from Geb and retreat to the sky records the rise of more patriarchal attitudes.

---

101. see Hollis 1994: 87
102. Lesko 1999
103. Spell I ff, 427ff

She shares some characteristics of other primal bovine Goddess such as Hathor, or also Mehet-Weret ("The Great Flood"). One of her oldest names/epithets is Bat meaning "female soul" or "female power" which according to Barbara Lesko signifies the deification of the essence of femininity. Another name is "Kha-bawes" : "one with a thousand souls." (Cerny). Bat is the old sky Goddess of Nekhen ("Citadel of the Hawk") and is also sometimes paired with Lord Seth, the *Bull of Ombos*.

The largest representations of Nuit, indeed any deity in Egypt are to be found in the first hypostyle hall of the temple of Hathor at Dendara. Dendara is the main cult centre of the Cow Goddess Hathor. Nuit's appearance at Dendara underlines the fact that she has no exclusive cult centre in her own right. She is invariably worshipped in a small chapel in association with another God or Goddess. This does not detract from her status but is the natural consequence of her chthonic, otherworld role.

As time went by Nuit become part of the so-called mortuary cult in which she is the personification of the coffin. The coffin can be viewed as a stylised *womb*. Wrapped inside this womb, the deceased waits to be reborn after a long period of incubation.

> "Oh my mother Nuit, stretch yourself over me, that I
> may be placed amongst the imperishable stars, which are
> in you, and that I may not die." [104]

---

104. From a New Kingdom coffin in tomb of Hattiay at Thebes, the singer of Amon henut-wadjebu now in Cleveland Museum of Art No 61

The sycamore is a tree sacred to Hathor. However because the wood was commonly used to make coffins, Nuit can also appear in this tree.

The female sky is the realm of the dead, whereas the Earth is for the living. This perhaps explains the male rulership of the Earth. In other cultures the movement of time and space was a role ascribed to male deities such as Marduk, Yahweh, or Mithras. In ancient times before the patriarchal religions, great Goddesses may well have taken a more central role in this.

When the Sungod Ra travels across the sky he travels *through* Nuit. The language "winding waterway", "nurse canal", "field of reeds" "doors thrown open" is very visceral, deliberately so. Aleister Crowley intuitively used the same kind of language when describing life's deeper mysteries. Nuit is unique in Egyptian art for being shown nude.[105] Her nakedness is partly erotic and also to do with the mysteries of birth. She gives birth to all the Gods, all the stars, so why not us?

One important aspect of Nuit, especially in Ramesside times is a connection with the God Seth. One of his most important epithets is "Son of Nuit". Now of course as mother of all the Gods this epithet could be taken by any. Even so it seems to be especially associated with Seth. This relationship is usually downplayed in studies of Nuit or relegated to the eccentricities of the Ramesside kings, well-known for their revival of the Sethian cult. Te Velde even says it is because of Seth's (allegedly) "Oedipal" nature! Whatever way you look at it the Queen Mother is a force to be reckoned with.

---

105. Lesko (1999)

Seth was often depicted in the presence of Nuit, for instance at the memorial chapel of Ramesses III at Medinat Habu. Interestingly she is here shown in her bovine form, a clear reference to ancient times when Nuit was the Heavenly Cow Goddess.

Top register of gatehouse at Medinet Habu, the exacrated figure is Seth, the accompanying inscription says the figure left of Seth is the Goddess Nuit.

THE BOOK OF NUIT

Nuit is intimately connected with the stars, especially those that are close to and appear to envelop our world. You may be familiar with the following image of Nuit at the moment of creation:

It shows a key moment in the unfolding of the cosmos as envisaged by the priests of Heliopolis. Just to remind you, in this system, creation begins with the ambisexual[106] Amun-Ra or Sungod Ra. He has the power to emanate parts of himself, creating other Gods and Goddesses. He starts with Shu and Tefnut - who represent the principles of air and fire respectively. The process of emanation continues and they generate Nuit the sky Goddess and Geb the Earth. Initially Nuit and Geb are locked together in a sexual embrace, almost a single entity. It is Shu, the God of the winds and the air who separates them, creating a space between all these elements in which our world can exist.

Nuit and Geb emanate their own generation of Gods, including Seth who remains especially close to Nuit. If this image is new to you then it repays some meditation. I have introduced the first layer of meaning but there is a lot more. This image is invariably accompanied by some very complex and indeed ancient astronomical texts.

---

106. His famous act of autoerotic creation encapsulates male and female
        motifs - masturbation/ejaculation (male) swallowing/birthing (female)

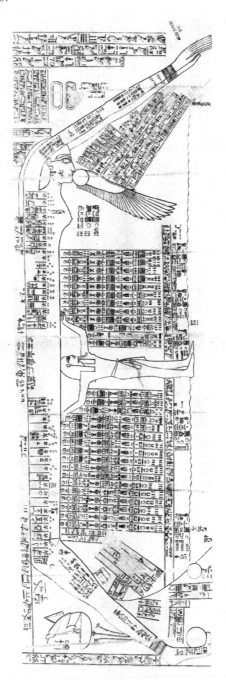

Astrological ceiling from roof of sarcophagus chamber, the Osireion, Abydos
(publication Frankfort, tracing Emery). Width 10.25meters. Orientation N-S

The image left is a more complete version. It is an astronomical ceiling from the temple of Sety I at Abydos. Look at the elongated body of Nuit, Geb (the floor) and Shu in the centre separating them. To the untrained eye a jumble of hieroglyphs are written all over the picture. This text was originally known by Egyptologists as *The Book of Nuit*. More recent research has uncovered the original if slightly less elegant title the *Book of the Fundamentals of the Course of the Stars*.[107]

The texts to the left indicated by the image of a falcon with a flail, concern the rising Sun; those to the extreme right the setting Sun. The large collection of vertical hieroglyphic text between Nuit and Geb concerns the "decans" of the visible stars (more of them in a moment). The vertical lines of hieroglyphs *inside* the body of Nuit, is another, much older system of decans, perhaps obsolete or concerned with an earlier lunar calendar.

The ancient Egyptians divided the year into 36 weeks of ten days each - hence "decan" from Greek "ten". The *Book of Nuit* tells us that the God Shu, personifies the wind, air and atmosphere. It is Shu who controls the ebb and flow of the decans. When the stars are visible at night the Egyptians saw them as metaphorically *outside* the body of Nuit. Thus when the stars are visible they are in the realm of Shu, who uses the four winds to direct their movement. Some images of Nuit show her surrounded by images of the four winds.

---

107. Leitz (1995 3-57) quoted in A S von Bomhard (2008)
     The Noas of the Decans, Oxford

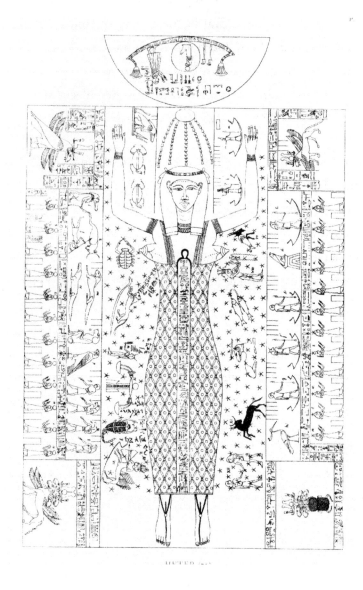

Coffin of Heter, from Neugebauer O & Parker, R (1962) *Ancient Egyptian Astronomical Texts*, 4 vols, Brown University. Now lost published by H Brugsch, *Recueil de monuments égyptiens dessinés sur lieux et publ. par H. Brugsch. [With] Geographische Inschriften altägyptischer Denkmäler, von J. Duemichen. 6 pt. [in 7].*

THE DECANS

"The snake is in my hand and cannot bite me" [108]

"Oh lion and serpent who destroys the destroyer,
be mighty among us" [109]

The iconography of the decans predates that of all famous European books of magick such as the *Testament of Solomon* or the *Goetia et al.* The spirits of all these texts are mostly malign.

Each week is ruled over by particular stars, rising in sucession over the course of a year. These can be observed rising on the eastern horizon just before dawn. The star rises by approximately one degree each day. After ten days a new decanal star appears. The old star continues its rise through the year, culminating in the "middle of the sky" (midheaven) then declining again to the west before disappearing from view.

Moving at the rate of one degree a day it takes about eight weeks to ascend to the middle of the sky. It will remain visible there for a further twelve weeks. Its final nine weeks will be descending slowly to the west before spending seven weeks in the "Underworld" and invisible to us.

You and I were born into this intricate web of stars. The 36 decans are in effect the earlier Egyptian equivalent of the later Greek system of twelve zodiac signs. The twelve *culminating* decans are also the equivalent of the twelve "houses".

---

108. Coffin Text 885 ancient words to ward off evil, quoted in Ritner (1993)
109 Aleister Crowley (1973) 'Gnostic Mass" in *Magick: Liber ABA,* Routledge

The Book of Nuit is a snapshot of the sky at one particular moment in time. The monument itself dates from the time of Sety I of the 19th dynasty (circa 1350BCE). But it is actually a picture of the sky from the earlier time when Egypt was first unified circa 3300BCE! The hieroglyphs within the body of Nuit are even older. These particular moments in time were obviously of special importance and they recur on Egyptian monuments again and again.

The very famous circular astronomical ceilings from Dendara, especially Dendera B now in the Louvre, uses the native system of decans as well as the Greco-Babylonian signs of the zodiac. The Egyptian decans were eventually absorbed into the Greek system. The Egyptians accepted many new Babylonian and Greek astrological ideas. But in the case of the 36 decans they could insist on the priority of their own native system. The decans continue to be an important aspect of tropical astrology, its Egyptian legacy.

In Egyptian star-lore, "horoscopes" tend to document the negatives present at a person's birth. The use of astrology would presage that of later "tantrik" attitudes. This is knowledge that might be helpful to *decondition* oneself and to *avoid* fate. It is about wiping one's name from the great *Book of Fate*. The emissaries of Shu or of Hathor, also known as the Hateyew (*h3tyw*) are similar to what we think of as daemons. They are sent to reap a sinister harvest of humanity. They act on the basis of these "reports" in the Book (of Calamities). So best to know what is in that book and if possible erase the entry! [110]

---

110. See A S von Bomhard *(2008) The Noas of the Decans*, Oxford

As an aid to this process here is a popular list of decans along with their meanings where known. This is a rough guide. You will have to supplement this with data drawn from your own experience as well as updates and revisions from the Ombos website connected with this book. If you check online you will find I calculate the months for the current lunar year of writing. Subsequent years can be seen in skeletal form on my website and are available on request.

How to use this emphemeris:

What follows is essentially an ephemeris charting the relationship between Egyptian "daemons" and the year. I have given approximate dates from the modern calendar in brackets. The most obvious personal relationship would be those daemons that are connected with one's birth. Daemons aspecting one's birthday are said to be particularly special and personal. This knowledge is important as an insight into fate as well as your guardian spirit. Secondarily to this one might also review daemons as they arise on other special days in one's life. All this information is approximate, for a more precise calculation of your birth daemons and prognosis, the reader is encouraged to follow links on the Ombos website or contact the author directly for advice.

Note on illustrations

As the records upon which the following are based are quite old, often fragmentary and inconsistent, there is an occasional mismatch between the description and the illustration. Thus the first entry is the Goddess Isis with feather crown representing the star Sothis. The corresponding drawing does not quite match the description because the ancient artist was working from a different script. The keen eyed may also notice that some hieroglyphic captions sometime do not quite match the translation. This ephemeris is a good approximation from several sources. Likewise, where there are lacunae in the original I have substituted a version from another inscription. The ancients were also familiar with incomplete omen texts, which over time were corrected on the basis of experience. Thus if you happen to be born on a day where the information is missing, but have a reasonably good life (or vice versa) then the meaning of this day can be inferred.

(1) AKHET I.1
(22 JUL-31 AUG)[111]

Rulership:

Sothis (*sepedet*).

Image

Goddess Isis with feather crown

Mineral:

Gold or Lapis Lazuli

Aspects:

Day 1   FFF

Day 2   FFF

Day 3   FFA

Day 4   FFA

Day 5   FFF

Day 6   AAF

Day 7   FFF

Day 8   FFA

Day 9   FFF

Day 10 FFF

Abramelin:

Morech, Serep, Proxone, Nablum, Kosem,

Peresh, Thirana, Aluph, Neschamah, Milon,

---

111. All the following correspondences are based on the so-called Sety I B
family of decans as described in Neugebauer & Parker (1960) *Egyptian
Astronomical Texts, vol III Decans, Constellations and Zodiacs.* The aspects are

(2) Aкнет I.2
(1st - 10th Aug)

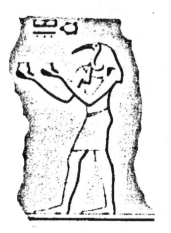

Rulership:

Setew (*št(w)*)

Image:

Ibis or serpent headed God, standing, offering two nw-jars.

Mineral:

Carnelian and gold

Aspect:

Day 1   AAA

Day 2   AAA

Day 3   FAA

Day 4   [unknown]

Day 5   FAA

Day 6   AAA

Day 7   AAA

Day 8   FFF

Day 9   FFF

Day 10 AAA

Abramelin:

Frasis, Haja, Malacha, Molabeda, Yparcha,

Nudatoni, Methaera, Bruahi, Apollyon, Schaluah,

---

taken from *The Cairo Calendar* (1960) translation by Abd el-Mohsen Bakir (actually more of an Almanac than a calendar). See earlier discussion for the arrangement of Abramelin daemons.

(3) AKHET I.3
(11 AUG - 20TH AUG)

Rulership:
Kenemet (*knm(t)*)

Image:
Erect serpent with three smaller serpents

Mineral:
Garnet

Aspect:
Day 1   FFF

Day 2   AAA

Day 3   AAA

Day 4   FFF

Day 5   FFA

Day 6   AAA

Day 7   FFF

Day 8   FFF

Day 9   AFF

Day 10 FFF

Abramelin:
Myrmo, Melamo, Pother, Schad, Echdulon,
Manmes, Obedomah, Iachil, Ivar, Moschel,

(4) AKHET II.1
(21ST - 30TH AUG)

Rulership:

Khery kheped kenemet

(*ḥry ḫpd knm(t)*)

Image:

lion-headed Goddess, uraeus or disk
on head, seated, scepter & ankh.

Mineral:

Glass and gold

Aspect:

Day 1 FFF

Day 2 [unknown]

Day 3 FFF

Day 4 AFA

Day 5 AAA

Day 6 FFF

Day 7 A

Day 8 FFF

Day 9 FFF

Day 10 FFF

Abramelin:

Peekah, Hasperim, Kathim, Porphora, Badet,
Kohen, Lurchi, Falfuna, Padidi, Helali,

(5) AKHET II.2
(31ST SEP - 9TH OCT)

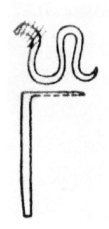

Rulership:

Heset djat (*hst ḏ3t*)

Image:

Serpent on a support

Mineral:

Glass and Gold

Aspect:

Day 1   FFF

Day 2   AAA

Day 3   FFF

Day 4   FFF

Day 5   FAA

Day 6   [unknown]

Day 7   FFF

Day 8   [unknown]

Day 9   FFF

Day 10 AAA

Abramelin:

Mahra, Raschëa, Nogah, Adae, Erimites,
Trapi, Naga, Echami, Aspadit, Nasi,

(6) AKHET II.3
(10TH - 19TH SEP)

Rulership:

Phewy djat (*pḥwy ḏ3t*)

Image:

Erect serpent

Mineral:

Galena and Gold

Aspect:

Day 1   AAF

Day 2   AAA

Day 3   FAA

Day 4   [unknown]

Day 5   AAA

Day 6   AAA

Day 7   AAA

Day 8   FFF

Day 9   FFF

Day 10 FFF

Abramelin:

Peralit, Emfalion, Paruch, Girmil, Tolet,
Helmis, Asinel, Ionion, Asturel, Flabiscon,

(7) AKHET III.1
(20TH - 29TH SEP)

Rulership:

Temat heret kheret (*tm3t hrt ḫrt*)

Image:

Lion-headed Goddess,

Uraeus or disk on head,

seated, scepter & ankh.

Mineral:

Glass and Gold

Aspect:

Day 1 FFF

Day 2 [unknown]

Day 3 FFF

Day 4 AAA

Day 5 AAA

Day 6 FFF

Day 7 FFF

Day 8 [unknown]

Day 9 AAA

Day 10 FFF

Abramelin:

Nascela, Conioli, Isnirki, Pliroki, Aslotama,

Zagriona, Parmasa, Sarasi, Geriola, Afonono,

(8) AKHET III.2
(30TH SEP - 9TH OCT)

Rulership:

Weshatei bekati (*wš3t(i) bk3t(i)*)

Image:

a serpent with human arms and legs, standing, offering two nw-jars.

Mineral:

Turquoise

Aspect:

Day 1 FFF

Day 2 [unknown]

Day 3 AAA

Day 4 AAA

Day 5 AAA

Day 6 FFF

Day 7 AAA

Day 8 AAA

Day 9 AAA

Day 10 AAA

Abramelin:

Liriell, Alagill, Opollogon, Carubot, Morilon, Losimon, Kagaros, Ygilon, Gesegos, Ugefor,

(9) Akhet III.3
(10th - 19th oct)

Rulership:

Ipesed or ipedejs *(Ipsd, ipds)*

Image:

Erect serpent

Mineral:

Iron and gold

Aspect:

Day 1 FFF

Day 2 [unknown]

Day 3 AAA

Day 4 FFF

Day 5 FFF

Day 6 FFF

Day 7 FFF

Day 8 FFF

Day 9 FFF

Day 10 FFF

Abramelin:

Asoreg, Paruchu, Siges, Atherom, Ramara,
Jajaregi, Golema, Kiliki, Romasara, Alpaso,

(10) Akhet IV.1
(20th - 29th Oct)

Rulership:

Sebeshsen or sebehes (*sbšsn, sbḥs*)

Image: :

Lion-headed Goddess, Uraeus or disk on head,
seated with two flagella

Mineral:

Glass and Gold

Aspect

Day 1 FFF

Day 2 FFF

Day 3 AAA

Day 4 FFF

Day 5 FFF

Day 6 AAA

Day 7 AAA

Day 8 FFF

Day 9 FFF

Day 10 FFF

Abramelin:

Soteri, Amillee, Ramage, Pormatho, Metosee,
Porascho, Anamil, Orienell, Timiran, Oramos,

(11) Akhet IV.2
(30th oct - 8th nov)

Rulership:

Tepy-'khenet (*tpy-ꜥḫnt*)

Image:

human headed Goddess with outstretched arms, as though seated but with no support

Mineral:

Haematite

Aspect:

Day 1 FFF

Day 2 AAA

Day 3 FFF

Day 4 FFF

Day 5 [unknown]

Day 6 [unknown]

Day 7 AAF

Day 8 AAA

Day 9 AAA

Day 10 AAA

Abramelin:

Anemalon, Kirek, Batamabub, Ranar, Namalon, Ampholion, Abusis, Egention, Tabori, Concario,

(12) Akhet IV.3
(9th - 18th nov)

Rulership:

Khenetet horet (*ẖnt(t) ḥr(t)*)

Image:

Erect serpent

Mineral:

Dark Quartz and Gold

Aspect:

Day 1 AAF

Day 2 FFF

Day 3 FFA

Day 4 [unknown]

Day 5 [unknown]

Day 6 ??F

Day 7 FFA

Day 8 AAA

Day 9 AAA

Day 10 FFF

Abramelin:

Golemi, Tarato, Tabbata, Buriuh, Omana,
Caraschi, Dimurga, Kogid, Panfodra, Siria,

(13) PERET 1.1
(19TH - 28TH NOV)

Rulership:

Khenetet kheret (ḫnt(t) ḫrt)

Image:

Lion-headed Goddess, Uraeus on head, seated with sistrum and flagellum. Or lion-headed God, standing, hands on heads of two monkeys squatted on supports.

Mineral:

Red jasper and gold

Aspect:

Day 1 FFF
Day 2 F
Day 3 ???
Day 4 FFF
Day 5 FAA
Day 6 FFF
Day 7 AAA
Day 8 FFF
Day 9 FFF
Day 10 AAA

Abramelin:

Igigi, Dosom, Darachin, Horomor, Ahahbon, Yraganon, Lagiros, Eralier, Golog, Cemiel,

(14) PERET 1.2
(29TH NOV - 8TH DEC)

Rulership:

Temen khenetet (*tmn ḫnt(t)*)

Image:

Lion headed God standing

Mineral:

Glass and Gold

Aspect:

Day 1 AAA

Day 2 AAA

Day 3 FFF

Day 4 AAA

Day 5 FFF

Day 6 FFF

Day 7 AAA

Day 8 FFF

Day 9 AAA

Day 10 AAA

Abramelin:

Hagus, Vollman, Bialode, Galago, Bagoloni,

Tmako, Akanejohano, Argaro, Afrei, Sagara,

(15) PERET 1.3
(9TH - 19TH DEC)

Rulership:

Sepety henewy, "singer" (*spt(y) ḫnwy*)

Image:

Erect serpent

Mineral:

Flint

Aspect:

Day 1   FFF

Day 2   FFF

Day 3   FFF

Day 4   FFF

Day 5   [unknown]

Day 6   AAA

Day 7   FFF

Day 8   FFF

Day 9   FFF

Day 10 FFF

Abramelin:

Ugali, Erimihala, Hatuny, Hagomi, Opilon,
Paguldez, Paschy, Nimalon, Horog, Algebol,

(16) PERET 2.1
(20TH - 29TH DEC)

Rulership:

Hery-ib wia (*ḥry-ib wiȝ*)

"who dwells in the middle of the sacred bark"

Image:

Lion-headed Goddess,

Mineral: :

Lapis Lazuli and Gold

Aspect:

Day 1 FFF

Day 2 FFF

Day 3 AAA

Day 4 FFF

Day 5 FFF

Day 6 AAA

Day 7 FFF

Day 8 FFF

Day 9 FFF

Day 10 AAA

Abramelin:

Rigolon, Trasorim, Elason, Trisacha, Gagolchon, Klorecha, Irachro, Pafessa, Amami, Camalo,

(17) Peret 2.2
(30th dec - 9th jan)

Rulership:

Seshemew (sšmw)

Image: :

Serpent with human arms and legs,
standing, offering two nw-jars.

Mineral:

Glass and Gold

Aspect:

Day 1   FFF

Day 2   FFF

Day 3   AAA

Day 4   AFF

Day 5   [unknown]

Day 6   [unknown]

Day 7   FFF

Day 8   AAA

Day 9   FAA

Day 10 AAA

Abramelin:

Taxae, Karase, Riqita, Schulego, Giria,
Afimo, Bafa, Baroa, Golog, Iromoni,

(18) PERET 2.3
(10TH - 18TH JAN)

Rulership:

Kenemew (*knm(w)*)

Image:

Uraeus serpent coiled on a support

Mineral:

Gold and Carnelian

Aspect:

Day 1   [unknown]

Day 2   FFF

Day 3   FFF

Day 4   AAA

Day 5   FFF

Day 6   [unknown]

Day 7   [unknown]

Day 8   FFF

Day 9   AAA

Day 10   AAA

Abramelin:

Pigios, Nimtrix, Herich, Akirgi, Tapum,
Hipolopos, Hosun, Garses, Ugirpon, Gomognu,

(19) PERET 3.1
(19TH - 28TH JAN)

Rulership:

Tepy asemed (*tpy ꜥsmd*)

Image:

Lion-headed Goddess, Uraeus on head, seated,
scepter and ankh.

Mineral :

Gold

Aspect:

Day 1 FFF

Day 2 FFF

Day 3 [unknown]

Day 4 FAA

Day 5 FFF

Day 6 FFF

Day 7 AAA

Day 8 FFF

Day 9 FFF

Day 10 AAA

Abramelin:

Argilo, Tardoe, Cepacha, Kalote, Ychniag,
Basanola, Nachero, Natolisa, Mesah, Mesadu,

(20) PERET 3.2
(29TH JAN - 7TH FEB)

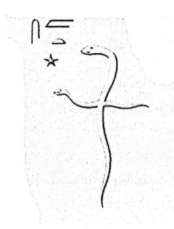

Rulership:

Semed (*smd*)

Image:

Erect serpent with another serpent
crossing its body

Mineral: :

Copper and Gold

Aspect:

Day 1 FFF

Day 2 FFF

Day 3 FFF

Day 4 AA

Day 5 AAA

Day 6 AAA

Day 7 AAA

Day 8 FFF

Day 9 [unknown]

Day 10 AAA

Abramelin:

Capipa, Fermetu, Barnel, Ubarim, Urgivoh,
Ysquiron, Odac, Rotor, Arator, Butharusch,

(21) PERET 3.3
(8TH - 17TH FEB)

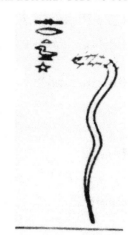

Rulership:

Seret (*srt*)

Image :

Erect serpent

Mineral:

Dark Flint and Gold

Aspect:

Day 1 FFF

Day 2 AAA

Day 3 FFF

Day 4 AAA

Day 5 [unknown]

Day 6 AAA

Day 7 AAA

Day 8 FFF

Day 9 FFF

Day 10 [unknown]

Abramelin:

Harkinson, Arabim, Koreh, Forsterton, Sernpolo,

Magelucha, Amagestol, Sikesti, Mechebbera, Tigrapho,

(22) PERET 4.1
(18TH - 27TH FEB)

Rulerhship:

Sa seret (*s3 srt*)

Image:

Lion-headed Goddess, Uraeus on head, seated, scepter and ankh

Mineral :

Carnelian and Gold

Aspect:

Day 1   FFF

Day 2   FFF

Day 3   AAA

Day 4   FFF

Day 5   AAA

Day 6   AAA

Day 7   FFF

Day 8   FFF

Day 9   AAA

Day 10 [unknown]

Abramelin:

Malata, Tagora, Petuna, Amia, Somi,
Lotogi, Hyris, Chadail, Debam, Abagrion,

(23) PERET 4.2
(28TH FEB - 9TH MAR)

Rulerhship:
Hery heped seret (*ḥry ḥpd srt*)

Image:
Erect winged serpent

Mineral:
Glass and Gold, sometimes Silver

Aspect:
Day 1   AAA

Day 2   AAA

Day 3   AAA

Day 4   AAA

Day 5   FFF

Day 6   FFF

Day 7   AAA

Day 8   AAA

Day 9   FFF

Day 10 AAA

Abramelin:
Paschan, Cobel, Arioth, Panari, Caboneton,
Kamual, Erytar, Nearah, Hahadu, Charagi,

(24) PERET 4.3
(10TH -19TH MARCH)

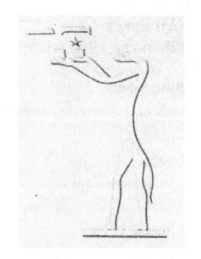

Rulership:

Tepy-Akhw (*tpy- ʿȝḫw*)

Image:

Serpent with human legs, standing

Mineral:

Garnet and Gold

Aspect:

Day 1 AAA

Day 2 AAA

Day 3 AAF

Day 4 AAA

Day 5 AAA

Day 6 AAA

Day 7 FFF

Day 8 FFF

Day 9 FFF

Day 10 FFF

Abramelin:

Kolani, Kibigili, Corocana, Hipogo, Agikus,
Nagar, Echagi, Parachmo, Kosirma, Dagio

(25) SHEMU 1.1
(20TH - 29TH MAR)

Rulership:

Akhw (3ḫw)

Image:

Human headed God

Mineral :

Gold

Aspect:

Day 1 FFF

Day 2 AAA

Day 3 FFF

Day 4 AAA

Day 5 AAA

Day 6 FFF

Day 7 FFF

Day 8 AAA*

Day 9 FFF

Day 10 AAA

Abramelin:

Oromonas, Hagos, Mimosah, Arakuson, Rimog,
Iserag, Cheikaseph, Kofan, Batirunos, Cochaly,

---

* Substituted the missing section in Cairo mss from British Museum mss

(26) Shemu 1.2
(30th mar - 8th apr)

Rulership:
Tepey abawey (*tpy 3bʿw(y)*)

Image:
Human-headed, armless God with body ending in a crocodile's tail

Mineral :
Gold

Aspect:
Day 1 AAA *

Day 2 AAA

Day 3 -F-

Day 4 AAA

Day 5 AAA

Day 6 F - F

Day 7 [unknown]

Day 8 [unknown]

Day 9 FFF

Day 10 AAA

Abramelin:
Ienuri, Nephasser, Bekaro, Hyla, Eneki, Maggio, Abbetira, Breffeo, Ornion, Schaluach,

(27) Shemu 1.3
(9th- 18th Apr)

Rulership:

Baw(y) ($b^ʿw(y)$) (The twin Bas)

Image:

Erect serpent with up-curved tail

Mineral:

Gold and unknown substance connected with horses (and perhaps dogs)*

Aspect:

Day 1 AAA

Day 2 FFF

Day 3 FFF

Day 4 AAA†

Day 5 FFF

Day 6 FFF

Day 7 AAA

Day 8 FFF

Day 9 FFF†

Day 10 FFF

Abramelin:

Hillaro, Ybario, Altono, Armefia, Belifares,

Camalo, Corilon, Dirilisin, Eralicarison, Elipinon,

---

* *ṯsmd/śsmit*

† substituted the missing section in Cairo mss from British Museum mss

(28) SHEMU 2.1
(19TH - 28TH APR)

Rulership:

Hor tep nefer (*ḥr tp nfr*)

Image:

Lion-headed Goddess,
standing with scepter and ankh

Mineral:

Gold

Aspect:

Day 1 FFF

Day 2 [unknown]

Day 3 FFF

Day 4 AAA

Day 5 FFF

Day 6 FFF*

Day 7 AAA

Day 8 FFF

Day 9 FFF

Day 10 FFF

Abramelin:

Gariniranus, Sipillipis, Ergomion, Lotifar, Chimirgu,
Kaerlesa, Nadele, Baalto, Ygarimi, Akahimo,

* substituted the missing section in Cairo mss from British Museum mss

(29) Shemu 2.2
(29th apr - 8th may)

Rulership:

Khenetew kherew ($ḫnt(w)$ $ẖr(w)$)

Image:

Falcon headed God, standing offering two nw-jars

Mineral :

Red Jasper and Gold

Aspect:

Day 1 AAA

Day 2 FFF

Day 3 FFF

Day 4 FFF

Day 5 AAA

Day 6 FFF

Day 7 AAA

Day 8 AAA

Day 9 AAA

Day 10 AAA

Abramelin:

Golopa, Naniroa, Istaroth, Tedea, Ikon,

Kama, Arisaka, Bileka, Yromus, Camarion,

(30) SHEMU 2.3
(9TH - 18TH MAY)

Rulership:

Sa ked (*s3 ḳd*)

Image:

Serpent with human arms, sometimes legs, standing, offering two nw-jars.

Mineral :

Glass and Gold

Aspect:

Day 1 AAF

Day 2 AAA

Day 3 FFF

Day 4 FFF

Day 5 FFF

Day 6 AAA

Day 7 AAA

Day 8 FFF

Day 9 FFF

Day 10 FFF

Abramelin:

Jamaih, Aragor, Igakis, Olaski, Haiamon, Semechle, Alosom, Segosel, Boreb, Ugolog,

(31) SHEMU 3.1
(19TH - 28TH MAY)

Rulership:

Khaw (*ḫ3w*) ("flowers - blue lily")

Image:

Lion-headed Goddess, mummified, seated.

Mineral:

Carnelian and Gold

Aspect:

Day 1   FFF

Day 2   FFF

Day 3   AAA

Day 4   FFF

Day 5   AAA

Day 6   AAA

Day 7   AAA

Day 8   AAA

Day 9   FFF

Day 10 AAA

Abramelin:

Hadcu, Amalomi, Bilifo, Granona, Pagalusta,
Hyrmiua, Canali, Radina, Gezero, Sarsiee,

(32) Shemu 3.2
(29th may - 7th jun)

Rulership:

Aret (ʿrt)

Image:

Falcon headed God,
standing offering two nw-jars

Mineral:

Granite and Gold

Aspect:

Day 1 AAA

Day 2 FFF

Day 3 AAA

Day 4 AAA

Day 5 FFF

Day 6 AAA

Day 7 AAA

Day 8 AAA

Day 9 AAA

Day 10 AAA

Abramelin:

Soesman, Tmiti, Balachman, Gagison, Mafalach,
Zagol, Ichdison, Sumuram, Aglasis, Hachamel,

(33) Shemu 3.3
(8th - 17th Jun)

Rulership:

Remen hery (*rmn ḥry*)

Image:

Serpent with human arms and legs,
offering two nw-jars

Mineral :

Quartz and Gold

Aspect :

Day 1 FFF

Day 2 AAA

Day 3 AAA

Day 4 FFF

Day 5 FAF

Day 6 FFF

Day 7 AAA

Day 8 AAA

Day 9 FFF

Day 10 FFF

Abramelin:

Agasoly, Kiliosa, Ebaron, Zalones, Jugula,
Carahami, Kaflesi, Mennolika, Takarosa, Astolitu,

(34) SHEMU 4.1
(18TH - 27TH JUN)

Rulership:
Tjes arek (ṯs ꜥrk)

Image :
Lion-headed Goddess, seated with
sistrum and flagellum

Mineral:
Glass and Gold

Aspect:
Day 1 FFF
Day 2 FFF
Day 3 AAA
Day 4 AAF
Day 5 FFF
Day 6 AAA
Day 7 AAA
Day 8 AAA
Day 9 FFF
Day 10 FFF

Abramelin:
Merki, Anadi, Ekore, Rosora, Negani,
Cigila, Secabmi, Calamos, Sibolas, Forfasan,

(35) SHEMU 4.2
(28TH JUN - 7TH JUL)

Rulership:

Waret heret (*w⁽rt (hrt)*)

Image:

Crocodile-headed God offering two nw-jars

Mineral:

Gold

Aspect:

Day 1 AAA

Day 2 FFF

Day 3 FFF

Day 4 FFF

Day 5 AAA

Day 6 FFF

Day 7 FFF

Day 8 AAF

Day 9 FFF

Day 10 AAA

Abramelin:

Andrachor, Notiser, Filakon, Horasul, Saris,
Ekorim, Nelion, Ylemis, Calacha, Sapasani,

(36) SHEMU 4.3
(8TH - 18TH JUL)

Rulership:

Tepy-aspedet (*tpy-ᶜspdt*)

Image:

Erect serpent with human arms,
offering two nw-jars

Mineral:

Ebony and Gold

Aspect:

Day 1 FFF

Day 2 FFF

Day 3 AAA

Day 4 FFF

Day 5 FFF

Day 6 FAF

Day 7 AAA

Day 8 FFF

Day 9 FFF

Day 10 FFF

Abramelin:

Seneol, Charonthona, Carona, Regerio, Megalogi,
Irmana, Elami, Ramgisa, Sirigilis, Boria.

BOOKS OF THE NIGHTWORLD (DUAT)

The Corpus Hermeticum are a collection of texts written in the twilight years of Egyptian pharaonic culture. The Renaissance classical scholar Meric Casaubon dismissed the idea that they were the work of an ancient priest or demi God called Thoth. He correctly recognized their provenance as late Roman Egypt. Far from debunking, this vital time adds greatly to their meaning and significance. They are the last testament of Egypt, writing whilst it was increasingly caught in the triple net of Christianity, the Roman Empire and Islam. Many Egyptologists now view the "theurgy" of *The Corpus Hermeticum* as the final legacy of Egyptian religion.

So to end I wanted to reintroduce some of the older, mythological books of the Egyptian magical-religion, the font from which drank the authors of the *Corpus Hermeticum*. Popular studies on Egypt have made famous *The Book of the Dead* or *Book of Coming Forth by Day*. Less well known but perhaps more significant are a series of Underworld books such as *The Book of Gates* and *The Book of Caverns*. The sequence of Egyptian religious literature begins with the Pyramid texts, closely followed by the *Coffin Texts*. *The Book of Coming Forth by Day* is a compilation derived from these earlier books. Next in sequence of composition are the *Underworld Books*. Their secret location in royal tombs implies they were intended for the eyes of the initiated.

The *Book of the Dead* is not really a book in our understanding of the term. It is not a continual narrative, it's a compendium, in papyrus form, comprising linked spells offering practical help to the deceased. There are spells for provisioning (feeding) and protecting the dead as he or she makes their ascent from the grave to the heavenly realm. Early sections addressed the wish for family re-union in the afterlife. The deceased begins their journey at dawn and reached heaven in several distinct steps (see Spells 144-147). One of these steps is the compulsory appearance and judgement before Osiris.

The Underworld Books present an *occult* counterpart to the above. These are coherent, illustrated books, charting mysteries such as the fate of the "Sun at Midnight". The Egyptologist Erik Hornung describes them as religious phenomenon founded in the resurgent New Kingdom circa 1600BCE. Compositions such as *The Book of Caverns*, *The Book of Gates* and the *Book of What is in the Netherworld* share a new religious sensibility.

Copies of these books are painted on the famous tombs of various New Kingdom Pharaohs. Fine examples are found on the tomb of Sety I in the Valley of the Kings. And the entire *Book of Gates* is carved onto his wonderful, alabaster sarcophagus currently displayed in the John Soanes Museum, London. Another example, *The Book of Caverns*, is carved on the walls of his "mortuary temple" at Abydos. These locations lead one to deduce that they were protected from profane eyes. Jan Assmann says "they are codifications of cosmological knowledge that belonged to the solar cult and constituted the basis of its successful practice." [112]

All these books chart the nightly journey of the Sun from death at sunset to birth at Sunrise. The Sun's journey is also the odyssey of the soul. The Egyptian word for soul (Ba) is identical with the word for Ram - the iconic image of the Sun-God. The Sun-God is thus our guide and role model, through various times and situations in our life on the journey from Death to Life and Life to Death.

---

112. Assmann (2001 : 64)

Reading these books become a little easier when one takes account of ancient literary conventions. For example the "discourse" is arranged in "registers", most commonly three to represent the sacred river Nile between its two banks. The central register, as your might expect, is central. The activity on either bank is interesting but peripheral.

The beginning, middle and end of the journey are priviledged moments. At midnight the sun faces a difficult ordeal. He is reunited with his "corpse" which perhaps represents the memory of his/her previous self. Assisted by the God Seth he must overcome the serpent Apophis, "demon of non-being". The famous God Osiris may make an appearance but is always passive and never speaks.

The *Book of Caverns* envisions this journey as the traversing of six spaces or caverns of the underworld. The *Book of Gates* charts the same journey as it progresses in time through the 12 "hours" of the night. The *Book of What is in the Netherworld* maps it in terms of movement of the constellations. It is the same journey with different maps.

The average Egyptian found many of these ideas challenging and difficult to comprehend. Special edited versions were produced for the perplexed or struggling. A whole class of mythological papyri is almost entirely pictorial with text kept to a bare minimum. The heart of the matter can be reduced to a handful of mythological scenes.

Here is one famous episode from one of those pictorial versions:[113]

---

113. Alexandre Piankoff (1974) *Egyptian religious texts and representations,* Vol 4, Mythological papyri (Papyrus Her-Uben B) Bollingen

One can focus on a particular version as preparation for the inevitable journey. I suggest each of us would benefit from the drawing up of a personalized version of that scroll. This could encapsulate traditional elements together with personal insights from research but also dreams, memories and reflections that are sure to assail you when you undertake this task. The selection of Egyptian liturgy below includes my own rendition of the *Book of Gates*.

THE BOOK OF GATES
A PROSE ARRANGEMENT [114]

I suggest this could be read during the 12 hours of the night or the night watch. The journey through the mountains of the East and West is something achievable in life and indeed at death. If the latter then these lines could be used during the long night before the burial or cremation and over the coffin of the deceased or perhaps addressed to a death mask or photograph (the modern equivalent).

You who came into being from Re, from his Glorious Eye.
Granted to you is a hidden seat in the Desert.

Come together all those created by the Gods.
The God has taken your measure in the Necropolis.

114. Alexandre Piankoff (1974) *Egyptian religious texts and representations*, 6 vols, Bollingen : 154

As he does for all those living on this Earth;
created as it is, from his right eye, the Sun.

The desert is bright,
I give it light,
With what is in me.

Souls of the West, those who would destroy humanity,
my glorious Eye is on you.

I have ordered the destruction, destruction of the enemies of Ra;
of the enemies of those upon the Earth, where the chosen ones are.

Breath be given to you, among whom I am
Let there be rays for you, dweller in the *region of offerings*.

To you is restored the diadem in the desert.
To you is restored the diadem in the necropolis.

The Gods shall say:
"Your presence is commanded by the great God,
He who lifts up his arms and moves his legs; as shall you,
Come to us, you who share his essence; and say
Hail to the One in His disk, Great God with numerous forms."

1ˢᵗ Gate

At the first gate, a large serpent stands
His name *guardian of the desert* is upon the door.
He opens for Ra, and those upon the Earth,
Full with the chosen ones of the Gods.

Your mind as a God speaks, from the prow of the sun-boat
Saying to the wise serpent: *Guardian of the Desert,*

"Open the Netherworld for Ra,
Open the door for the *One of the Horizon.*
The Hidden Chamber is in darkness,
Waiting for him to create his forms anew."

You and the God sail through,
On the winding waterway,
The great door closes after you,
which makes the dead souls wail.

2nd Gate

Sentiments drift, an hour already, floating in the Hidden Chamber,
You are at the second gate of the night,
guarded by the wise serpent,
the one called *The encircler.*

"Open the gate", call the Gods,
"For the One of the Horizon, has arrived; throw open the door,
For those who are in heaven, Hail, come, let them pass
travelling in the west."

"Open the door", my mind says:
"Open the door for Ra,
throw open the door for the One of the Horizon,
where he lightens the complete darkness,
and makes the Hidden Chambers bright."
You and the God sail through

On the winding waterway,

The great door closes after you,

which makes the dead souls wail.

3rd Gate

The great serpent of time unravels, the hours before, the hours to come,

The trembling centre of the Earth, where earthquakes live.

A hungry ghost, slipping deeper, deeper in the primal waters,

An ocean of souls, a sea of story, folding and unfolding before & after.

Mistress of food is the name on the gate, she opens the earth,

guarded by the spitting cobras, those who light for Ra, the sun God.

The Gods say, "You have opened the earth,

You have opened the door, O Heavenly One,

Ra uncovers those who are in darkness,

Hail, Sun God, come to us"

Mind says to Serpent, *Stinging One*, who sits upon the gate,

"Open for Ra,

throw open the Netherworld for the *One of the Horizon*,

While he lightens the complete darkness,

and makes the Hidden Chamber bright."

You and the God sail through,

On the winding waterway,

The great door closes after you,

which makes the dead souls wail.

4th Gate

Jackals circle and prowl, on a gate called *She who acts,*
Warmed by the wise serpent, *Flame Face* guards the door.

The company of heaven say: "Let us open for Ra,
Throw open our gate for *Horus of the Horizon.*
Hail Ra, Come to us, Great God, Lord of Hidden things"

Your mind as a God speaks, from the prow of the sun God's-boat,
"Open the door, open for the *One of the Horizon,*
Let him lighten the complete darkness,
and make the Hidden Chamber bright."

You and the God sail through,
On the winding waterway,
The great door closes after you,
which makes the dead souls wail.

5th Gate

Twelve Gods stand on the outer wall, *Mistress of Duration*'s gate,
In the Judgement Hall of Osiris, Gods and Goddesses call out.

"Come to us. He at the Head of the Horizon,
Great God, Light of the Earth,
May thou open the Holy Gates,
throw wide the two mysterious Doors."

In the crenulated Hall, nine steps lead to a throne,
where a sovereign weighs, your whole life in his hands.
On every step a God, Behold your life in the balance,

Through all its phases, Rising, culminating and decline.

A confusion of images, Four antelope heads look down,
Anubis broods, monkeys sailing, pigs fly by.
Shepherded by a baboon, wielding a crooked staff,
Steady your heart to say:
"Never did I do any bad thing against the people!"

You and the God sail through,
On the winding waterway,
The great door closes after you,
which makes the dead souls wail.

6th Gate

You fair, united, through a gate called *seat of her lord*,
Guarded by a Serpent, *He whose eye roves about*.

Mind says: "Open the door for Ra,
throw open thy door for the *One of the Horizon*,
He lightens the complete darkness,
and makes the Hidden Chamber bright."

You and the God sail through,
On the winding waterway,
The great door closes after you,
which makes the dead souls wail.

7th Gate

At the seventh gate things come together,
brightness at the end of the tunnel.

All downstream to *The Brilliant One*,

guarded by *Closed eyes* serpent.

He is blind and cannot see you,

Or anything you lack.

Mind says;

"Open the Netherworld for Re,

throw open thy door for the One of the Horizon,

he lightens the complete darkness,

and makes the Hidden Chamber Bright."

You and the God sail through,

On the winding waterway,

The great door closes after you,

which makes the dead souls wail.

8ᵗʰ Gate

The eighth gate is *Glowing*, the guardians you embrace

Your heart with emotion overflows, you remember *Flame Face*,

The wise serpent is familiar,

His warmth feels so good.

Open the door for Ra,

throw open the door for the One of the Horizon,

he lightens the complete darkness,

and makes the Hidden chamber bright.

You and the God sail through,

On the winding waterway,

The great door closes after you,

Which makes the dead souls wail.

9th Gate

The ninth door is called, the *Gate of Honour,*
Guarded by the Serpent: *Horn of the Earth.*

The outgrowing of the earth, the joy of rising up,
Encompassing, supporting, the life force coming back,
Mind says: "Open the door for Re,
throw open thy door for the One of the Horizon,
He lightens the complete darkness,
and makes the Hidden chamber bright."

You and the God sail through,
On the winding waterway,
The great door closes after you,
Which makes the dead souls wail.

10th Gate

At the tenth gate, you see more on the lintel,
The company of heaven, changed to twenty four cobras,
But you fear them not, the upper guardian with his knife of flint,
you know his name *executioner*, impostor you are not.

You have passed the lower regions, know the names of all,
The Uniter is the wise serpent, things are coming together.

Minds says:
"Open the Netherworld of Ra, throw open thy door.
He lightens the complete darkness,
and makes the Hidden Chamber bright."

You and the God sail through,

On the winding waterway,

The great door closes after you,

which makes the dead souls wail.

11th Gate

The eleventh gate is clearer still, its name *Mysterious of Approaches*,

Guarded by the Serpent, *The One in his discharge.*

On the lintel two sceptres rest, capped by the heads,

Of father and son, Horus and Osiris.

Each wears the red crown, of the south the sceptres say:

"Peace thou whose forms are numerous,

Peace thou whose forms are numerous."

The old body is gone, cut away from you by the knives

of the cutting one, what remains is the crowned head.

Your soul is in heaven,

your body in the earth,

greatness has been ordained,

by your very own self.

Mind says: "Open the Netherworld of Ra, throw open thy door,

He lightens the complete darkness,

he gives light to the *Chamber of Purity* (wabet)."

You and the God sail through,

On the winding waterway,

The great door closes after you,

which makes the dead souls wail.

12th Gate

After your long night, the final gate is here,
She whose power is holy, two pillars with human heads.

They face each on each, Atum the setting sun,
Kephra rising, coming, the beginning with the end.

Through twin doors of the horizon, it is the dawn,
When holy serpents fly and two cobras rest.

Isis & her sister Nephthys, those who light for Ra,
going after this God, into the mysterious Door of the West.

Mind says to a serpent at the door, the *One of the Morning*,
You who open for Ra. "Open the gate,
throw open the door, for the One of the Horizon,
for he comes out of the mysterious region,
to rest upon the body of Nuit."

Minds says to the *Encircler*, You upon the door:
"Open the gate for Ra, open for *The One of the Horizon*,
for he comes out of the mysterious region,
to move over the body of Nuit."

You and the God sail through
On the winding waterway
The great door closes one last time
which makes the dead souls wail.

Come out into the light, and contemplate death and birth,
The eternal sun, towed by eight Gods of earth.

On the sun boat of the morning, lifted by the Abyss
Abysmal waters surging up, from the faraway world.
Kephra the sacred scarab,
As new sun born through the eastern mountains
Isis and Nephthys bearing him up,
to the waiting Goddess of the sky.

Who stands above earthly sphere,
out of the old and into the new,
You are lifted into her arms,
Mother of the Gods, Nuit.

The Egyptian Liturgy

DRAWING DOWN THE PLOUGH

Whenever I have need of you
I draw down The Plough
Standing under the night stars,
The canopy clear above me
Searching the heavens for your sign,
An ox moving widdershins,
Tethered to a mast of flint
In the northern part of the sky

First I rouse your mate
Who lies sleeping in the earth beneath
Stamping the ground,
So Bat for Bata will awake
Tremors below rising through me
A conduit for the seething cauldron
As the power rises to my belly
My arms upwards piercing the barrier
Separating I and thou

And down it flows
that thing
into me,
or my cup
or via me to my companion
Dizzy now with the elixir
I follow your movements backwards
to the nameless aeon
when none ruled but I

OPENING: (REVISED VERSION)

Hekas, Hekas, Este Babaloi

"Love and do what you will"

Face North and try to see the constellation
Ursa Major.
Draw down its power and say:

0. Guardians of the House of Life at Abydos
   Before me in the East: Nephthys
   Behind me in the West, Isis
   On my right hand in the South is Seth
   And on my left hand, in the North, Horus
   For above me shines the body of Nuit
   And below me extends the ground of Geb
   And in my centre abideth the 'Great Hidden God'

Mnemonic:
[FAther GEt GAme to FEEd the HOt NEw hOme]

1. Now turn to the East.

   Make the "Horus Fighting" gesture.

   [Breath in and in one perfect movement, form both hands into fists
   and raise them up and to the left of your head, stretch your right
   hand and arm in front of you and bring the left hand and arm to join
   it. As you finish the intonation, bring both hands back to the centre
   of your body]

   Vibrate the first vowel long and hard - AAAAAAA - as in fAther

2. Now turn to the North

Make the gesture "Horus Fighting" and vibrate the second vowel
EEEEEEE, E as in gEt as above.

3. Then turn to the West

    Make the "Horus Fighting" gesture
    and vibrate ÊÊÊÊÊÊÊ, Ay as in GAme

4. Turn to the South

    Make the "Horus Fighting" gesture
    and vibrate IIIIIII, EE as in fEEd

5. Return to face the East

    Now bend over and reach out to the Earth
    vibrating OOOOOOO, as in HOt

6. Then gradually unfolding, come up and place your hands
    on your heart and vibrate YYYYYYY - Ew as in NEw

7. Finally stretching up to the heavens
    vibrate Ô Ô Ô Ô Ô Ô Ô O as in HÔme.

    Now make the sign of the (invoking) pentagram in the air
    in front of you and vibrate

        Aa, Eye, EE, Ou, Uh (Ay EAO - Oh Hail) Nephthys
        Aa, Eye, EE, Ou, Uh (Ay EAO - Oh Hail) Horus
        Aa, Eye, EE, Ou, Uh (Ay EAO - Oh Hail) Isis
        Aa, Eye, EE, Ou, Uh (Ay EAO - Oh Hail) Seth
        Aa, Eye, EE, Ou, Uh (Ay EAO - Oh Hail) Geb
        Aa, Eye, EE, Ou, Uh (Ay EAO - Oh Hail) Nuit
        Aa, Eye, EE, Ou, Uh (Ay EAO - Oh Hail) Hidden God

8. Repeat "Abydos Arrangement" (0)

POSSIBLE LINES FOR
DRAWING DOWN THE MOON

I draw down the bright blue Moon from the sky
though brazen cymbals crash and thunder
to keep her in her place;
even the chariot of the Sun,
my grandfather, grows pale at my song,
and I drain the colour from the dawn for my potions.[115]

---

115. Ovid: "Invocation of Hekate"

A GRECO-EGYPTIAN DICE ORACLE

The popular activity of cartomancy or divination by cards is a fairly modern innovation perhaps only two centuries old. Before this other methods were used which included geomancy and dice. Ancient dice might have six or four sides. The following Homer oracle was found in Egypt amongst the famous Theban Magical Library (PGM VIII 1-148). It needs three six-sided dice or one to be cast three times. Having conceived a query cast the dice - noting the resulting throws and then consulting the appropriate responses, all drawn from the works of Homer, the wandering bard whose cult was popular in Ptolemaic Egypt.

PGM VII 1-148

1-1-1   But on account of their accursed bellies they have miserable woes, [Od. 15. 344]

1-1-2   neither to cast anchor stones nor to attach stern cables, [Od. 9. 137]

1-1-3   being struck by the sword, and the water was becoming red with blood. [Il. 21. 21]

1-1-4   pick your man to be your companion, whichever you wish [Il. 10. 235]

1-1-5   stood holding a scepter, which Hephaistos produced by his labors. [Il. 2. 101]

1-1-6   Thus would murmur any man, Achaian or Trojan [Il. 4. 85]

1-2-1   amends I wish to make and to give a boundless ransom. [Il. 9. 120]

1-2-2   surely then the Gods have ruined your mind. [Il. 7. 360]

1-2-3 First, let their brains be spilled on the ground as this wine is spilled now [Il. 3. 300]

1-2-4 healing salves, by which he can put an end to the black pains [Il. 4. 191]

1-2-5 let it lie in the great hall. And I wish for your happy arrival. [Od. 15. 128]

1-2-6 Son of Atreus, give up your anger; even I entreat you [Il. 1. 282]

1-3-1 I myself will cast, and Zeus will look after the issue [Il. 17. 515]

1-3-2 On the twelfth day he will be coming back to Olympus [Il. 1. 425]

1-3-3 But Zeus does not accomplish for men all their purposes. [Il. 18. 328]

1-3-4 I would even wish it, and it would be much better [Il. 3. 41]

1-3-5 Then indeed would he smash all your fine show, [Od. 17. 244]

1-3-6 I also care about all these things, woman. But very terribly [Il. 6. 441]

1-4-1 And led them as spoil, but Zeus and the other Gods saved you [Il. 20. 194]

1-4-2 speaking good things, but they were contriving evil things in their hearts. [Od. 17. 66]

1-4-3 The glorious gifts of the Gods are surely not to be cast aside, [Il. 3. 65]

1-4-4 better had you never been born, or killed before you wed. [Il. 3. 40]

1-4-5 not in outright anger, and my meaning toward you is kindly. [Il. 8. 40]

1-4-6 These things, Zeus-nurtured Skamander, will be as you order. [Il. 21. 223]

1-5-1 a joy to your enemies and a disgrace to yourself? [Il. 3. 51]

1-5-2 Within this year, Odysseus will arrive here, [Od. 14. 161]

1-5-3 No use indeed to you, since you will not lie clad in them, [Il. 22. 513]

1-5-4 And to the victor are to go the women and the possessions. [Il. 3. 255]

1-5-5 The rule of the many is no good. Let there be one ruler, [Il. 2. 204]

1-5-6 And the gateway is full of ghosts, and full also is the courtyard, [Od. 20. 355]

1-6-1 We have won great honour. We have killed glorious Hektor, [Il. 22. 393]

1-6-2 Who would undertake and complete this task for? [Il. 10. 303]

1-6-3 Not even if his gifts to me should be as numerous as the grains of the sand and particles of dust, [Il. 9. 385]

1-6-4 I think they will not save you now, as your expectation [Il. 20. 195]

1-6-5 We should have called it a lie and we might rather have turned from it [Il. 2. 81]

1-6-6 And this shall be a thing of shame for the men hereafter. [Il. 2. 119]

2-1-1 For no island is made for driving horses or has broad meadows, [Od. 4. 607]

2-1-2 In the past, when you were boys, did you listen to your [Od. 4. 688]

2-1-3 Not that way, good fighter that you are, Godlike Achilles [Il. 19. 155]

2-1-4 Yes, old sir, all this you have said is fair and orderly. [Il. 1. 286]

2-1-5 Let me alone, then; Lord of the people, I am confounded [Il. 21. 221]

2-1-6 His gifts are hateful to me, and I honour him not a whit.

[Il. 9. 378]

2-2-1 An only beloved heir to many possessions, [Il. 9. 482]

2-2-2 If only he were somewhere on the sea, where the fish swarm [Il. 16. 746]

2-2-3 As east wind and south wind fight it out with each other [Il. 16. 765]

2-2-4 As when obliterating fire comes down on the timbered forest [Il. 11. 155]

2-2-5 So they thronged about him. And near [Od. 24. 19]

2-2-6 and fashioning lies out of what nobody could see. [Od. 11. 366]

2-3-1 be valiant, that later generations may also speak well of you. [Od. 1. 302]

2-3-2 leaning on the grave marker over a barrow heaped up by men [Il. 11. 371]

2-3-3 Go. You have a way, and beside the sea your ships [Il. 9. 43]

2-3-4 You will be proved a liar, and will not go on to fulfill your word. [Il. 19. 107]

2-3-5 And his mother for her part continued the lament amid a flood of tears, [Il. 22. 79]

2-3-6 Not even if remaining for five or six years [Od. 3. 115]

2-4-1 So he spoke, and ordered Paion to administer a cure. [Il. 5. 899]

2-4-2 These things, unhappy man, will I accomplish and do for you. [Od. 11. 80]

2-4-3 How can you propose to render toil useless and ineffectual? [Il. 4. 26]

2-4-4 a thing delayed, late of fulfillment, whose fame will never perish. [Il. 2. 325]

2-4-5 Sooner would you grow weary and return to your native land. [Od. 3. 117]

2-4-6 to go, that he may bring poisonous drugs from there, [Od. 2. 329]

2-5-1 Husband, you departed from life young, and me behind as a widow [Il. 24. 725]

2-5-2 in which way I will for sure accomplish everything and how it will be brought to pass, [Il. 9. 310]

2-5-3 Offer me not honey-tempered wine, honoured mother, [Il. 6. 264]

2-5-4 on that day when the Amazon women came, men's equals. [Il. 3. 189]

2-5-5 Be men now, dear friends, and take up the heart of courage. [Il. 5. 529]

2-5-6 Do not orphan your son and make your wife a widow. [Il. 6. 432]

2-6-1   Would that they might now eat their last and final meal here. [Od. 4. 685]

2-6-2   It is not meet for a man who speaks in the Council to sleep all the night through, [Il. 2. 24]

2-6-3   What's wrong with you, that you took this wrath into your heart? [Il. 6. 326]

2-6-4   But who knows if he will one day return and punish them for their violent deeds? [Od. 3. 216]

2-6-5   Wives I will provide for both and furnish possessions [Od. 21. 214]

2-6-6   We may try the bow and complete the contest. [Od. 21. 180]

3-1-1   For it's no reproach to flee evil, nor by night. [Il. 14. 80]

3-1-2   Be mindful of every form of valour. Now you needs must [Il. 22. 268]

3-1-3   As a widow at home. And the boy is still just a baby [Il. 24. 726]

3-1-4   But do in no wise enter the moil of Ares, [Il. 18. 134]

3-1-5   For amid misfortune mortals quickly grow old. [Od. 19. 360]

3-1-6   Lest he be hurt, and all their labour slip away into nothing [Il. 5. 569]

3-2-1   At that time when the dawn star passes across Earth, harbinger [Il. 23. 226]

3-2-2   Such a man is not alive nor will be born, [Od. 6. 201]

3-2-3   Of a truth, child, there's nothing really wrong with this, [Il. 18. 128]

3-2-4 Now is it no longer possible for him to find escape from us, [Il. 22. 219]

3-2-5 We will ransom with bronze and gold, for it is within. [Il. 22. 50]

3-2-6 Drink, and do not vie with younger men. [Od. 21. 310]

3-3-1 Where are you fleeing, turning your back like a craven in the ranks? [Il. 8. 94]

3-3-2 Would that such a man be called my husband [Od. 6. 244]

3-3-3 Plants her head in heaven and walks upon the Earth. [Il. 4. 443]

3-3-4 To him, a meaner father, was born a better son [Il. 15. 641]

3-3-5 And nodded for his army to survive and not to perish. [Il. 8. 246]

3-3-6 Would that you not plead with the noble son of Peleus, [Il. 9. 698]

3-4-1 Honey-sweet wine has the best of you, which others also [Od. 21. 293]

3-4-2 Act in whatever way your mind is moved, and no longer hold back. [Il. 22. 185]

3-4-3 For it is fated for both to turn the same ground red [Il. 18. 329]

3-4-4 Keep on shooting like this, if haply you may become a light to the Danaans [Il. 8. 282]

3-4-5 As there is no one who could keep the dogs off your head, [Il. 22. 348]

3-4-6 You will not kill me, since I am for sure not subject to Fate. [Il. 22. 13]

3-5-1 Staying right here you would help me watch over this house [Od. 5. 208]

3-5-2 Get out of the gateway, old man, or it won't be long before you're dragged out by the foot. [Od. 18. 10]

3-5-3 Better for a man to escape evil by flight than to be caught. [Il. 14. 81]

3-5-4 And declare to no one, neither man nor woman, [Od. 13. 308]

3-5-5 Of wheat or barley. And the heaps fall thick and fast. [Il. 11. 69]

3-5-6 Whatever sort of word you speak, such would you hear. [Il. 20. 250]

3-6-1 Was opposed to giving Helen to tawny Menelais, [Il. 11. 125]

3-6-2 Or will you alter your purpose? The hearts of the good are flexible. [Il. 15. 203]

3-6-3 Yet I for one never doubted, but at heart [Od. 13. 339]

3-6-4 Eurymachos, it will not be so. And even you know it. [Od. 21. 257]

3-6-5 You miserable foreigner, you have no sense at all. [Od. 21. 288]

3-6-6 And the father granted him one thing, but denied him the other. [Il. 16. 250]

4-1-1 Nay, go to your chambers and tend to your own work, [Od. 1. 356]

4-1-2 Now then, do not even tell this to your wife. [Od. 11. 224]

4-1-3 Would you have been stoned to death for all the wrongs you've done. [Il. 3. 57]

4-1-4 You prayed to the immortals to see with a beard grown. [Od. 18. 176]

4-1-5 And vow to Lycian-born Apollo the famous archer [Il. 4. 101]

4-1-6   And no spirit of harmony unites wolves and sheep, [Il. 22. 263]

4-2-1   Come now, let us make these concessions to one another, [Il. 4. 62]

4-2-2   And in the throng were Strife and Uproar, and Fate-of-Death, [Il. 18. 535]

4-2-3   Honor then the Gods, Achilles, and take pity on me [Il. 24. 503]

4-2-4   Up, rush into battle, the man you have always claimed to be. [Il. 4. 264]

4-2-5   Patroklos, and a huge loss is inflicted upon the Danaan [Il. 17. 690]

4-2-6   You baby, what use now to keep your bow idle? [Il. 21. 474]

4-3-1   For even fair-tressed Niobe turned her mind to food, [Il. 24. 602]

4-3-2   After giving a mass of bronze and gold and raiment [Od. 5. 38]

4-3-3   Surely then the journey will not be useless or fail to occur. [Od. 2. 273]

4-3-4   One omen is best, to defend your country. [Il. 12. 243]

4-3-5   I will gild her horns all round and sacrifice her to you. [Il. 10. 294]

4-3-6   And you would gain every Trojan's thanks and praise, [Il. 4. 95]

4-4-1   Put in with your ship since women are no longer trustworthy [Od. 11. 456]

4-4-2   It is not possible or proper to deny your request [Il. 14. 212]

4-4-3   Would straightaway fit his will to your desire and mine. [Il. 15. 52]

4-4-4   And give him instruction. And it will be beneficial for him to obey. [Il. 11. 789]

4-4-5 Will give glory to me, and your soul to horse-famed Hades. [Il. 5. 654]

4-4-6 Fill up his ship with gold and bronze aplenty, [Il. 9. 137]

4-5-1 But tell one part, and let the other be concealed. [Od. 11. 443]

4-5-2 And at birth Zeus sends a weight of misery. [Il. 10. 71]

4-5-3 Alone to have intelligence, but they are flitting shades. [Od. 10. 495]

4-5-4 Yielding to his indignation. But they now withheld from him the gifts [Il. 9. 598]

4-5-5 I rejoice at hearing what you say, son of Laërtes. [Il. 19. 185]

4-5-6 But Zeus causes men's prowess to wax or to wane, [Il. 20. 242]

4-6-1 A terrible man. He would be quick to blame even the blameless. [Il. 11. 654]

4-6-2 With all haste. For now would you capture the broad-wayed city [Il. 2. 66]

4-6-3 Endure now, my heart. An even greater outrage did you once endure, [Od. 20. 18]

4-6-4 You lunatic, sit still and listen to the word of others, [Il. 2. 200]

4-6-5 Had cast aside wrath and chosen friendship. [Il. 16. 282]

4-6-6 So good it is for a son to be left by a dead [Od. 3. 196]

5-1-1 Here then, spread under your chest a veil, [Od. 5. 346]

5-1-2 'Tis impiety to exult over men slain. [Od. 22. 412]

5-1-3 Through immortal night, when other mortals sleep? [Il. 24. 363]

5-1-4 How then could I forget divine Odysseus? [Od. 1. 65]

5-1-5 lurid death and o'erpowering death laid hold of [Il. 5. 83]

5-1-6 So there's nothing else as horrible and vile as a woman [Od. 11. 427]

5-2-1 Let us not advance to fight the Danaans around the shops. [Il. 12. 216]

5-2-2 to put up a defense when some fellow provokes a fight. [Il. 24. 369]

5-2-3 nor do children at his knees call him "papa" [Il. 5. 408]

5-2-4 I am this very man, back home now. And after many toils [Od. 21. 207]

5-2-5 Talk not like this. There'll be no change before [Il. 5. 218]

5-2-6 let him stay here the while, even though he's eager for Ares. [Il. 19. 189]

5-3-1 And do not, exulting in war and battle, [Il. 16. 91]

5-3-2 never to have gone to bed with her and had intercourse, [Il. 9. 133]

5-3-3 and moistens the lips but fails to moisten the palate. [Il. 22. 493]

5-3-4 Take heart! Let these matters not trouble your thoughts. [Il. 18. 463]

5-3-5 But this mad dog I'm unable to hit. [Il. 8. 299]

5-3-6 Keep quiet friend, and do as I say. [Il. 4. 412]

5-4-1 Bad deeds don't prosper. The slow man for sure overtakes the swift, [Od. 23. 7]

5-4-2 They shut fast and locked the doors of the hall. [Od. 21. 236]

5-4-3 Ah, poor man! Death's not at all on your mind, [Il. 17. 201]

5-4-4 Odysseus has come and reached home, though he was long in coming. [Od. 23. 7]

5-4-5 in full he will accomplish it at last, and the penalty they pay is great, [Il. 4. 161]

5-4-6 and therein was Strife, and therein Valor, and therein chilling Attack, [Il. 5. 740]

5-5-1 but 'tis most wretched to die and meet one's doom by starvation. [Od. 12. 342]

5-5-2 shall I be laid low when I die. But good repute is now my goal, [Il. 18. 121]

5-5-3 and the lion beats him down by force as he fights for his breath, so [Il. 16. 826]

5-5-4 In no way do I mock you, dear child, nor am I playing tricks. [Od. 23. 26]

5-5-5 but she stayed Alkmene's labor and stopped her from giving birth. [Il. 19. 119]

5-5-6 But come, and hereafter I shall make amends for this, if now anything wrong [Il. 4. 362]

5-6-1 Where are you two rushing? What cause the heart within your breast to rage? [Il. 8. 413]

5-6-2 Pray now, let him not be too much on your mind. [Od. 13. 421]

5-6-3 But the Gods do not, I ween, give men all things at the same time. [Il. 4. 320]

5-6-4 Talk not like this. There'll be no change before [Il. 5. 218]

5-6-5 So he spake, but did not move the mind of Zeus by saying this. [Il. 12. 173]

5-6-6 but Odysseus nodded no and checked him in his eagerness. [Od. 21. 129]

6-1-1 How can you want to go alone to the ships of the Achaians? [Il. 24. 203]

6-1-2 Then all the rest of the Achaians cried out in favor [Il. 1. 22]

6-1-3 And too, I've taken the mist from your eyes, which before was there, [Il. 5. 127]

6-1-4 It does not become you to be frightened like any coward. [Il. 2. 190]

6-1-5 And I know that my arrival was longed for by you two [Od. 21. 209]

6-1-6 I shall dress him in a mantle and a tunic, fine garments. [Od. 16. 79]

6-2-1 by fastening a noose sheer from a high rafter, [Od. 11. 278]

6-2-2 remembering our excellence, of the sort that even we [Od. 8. 244]

6-2-3 the sea's great expanse they cross, since this is the Earthshaker's gift to them. [Od. 7. 35]

6-2-4 Nay, come on with the bow. You'll soon be sorry for obeying everybody. [Od. 21. 369]

6-2-5 But hurry into battle and rouse the other soldiers. [Il. 19. 390]

6-2-6 For mighty Herakles, not even he escaped his doom, [Il. 18. 117]

6-3-1 amends I wish to make and to give a boundless ransom. [Il. 9. 120]

6-3-2 And let him stand up among the Argives and swear an oath to you [Il. 19. 175]

6-3-3   The man is nearby. Our search will not be long, if you are willing [Il. 14. 110]

6-3-4   and not quite suddenly, and a very God should be the cause? [Od. 21. 196]

6-3-5   Verily, these things have already happened, and not otherwise could be. [Il. 14. 53]

6-3-6   On now, follow close! In action numbers make a difference. [Il. 12. 412]

6-4-1   surely then the Gods themselves have ruined your mind. [Il. 7. 360]

6-4-2   Take heart, and let your thoughts not be of death. [Il. 10. 383]

6-4-3   by her wailing she roused from sleep her household servants, [Il. 5. 413]

6-4-4   Come now, in strict silence, and I shall lead the way, [Od. 7. 30]

6-4-5   are their ears for hearing, and sense and respect are dead. [Il. 15. 129]

6-4-6   as he was growing old. But the son did not grow old in his father's armor. [Il. 17. 197]

6-5-1   to return home and behold the day of homecoming. [Od. 5. 220]

6-5-2   Apollo of the silver bow did strike the one, still sonless, [Od. 7. 64]

6-5-3   then you may hope to see your loved ones and reach [Od. 7. 76]

6-5-4   soon you will bring to pass some still greater evil [Il. 13. 120]

6-5-5   For so shall I proclaim, and it will be accomplished too. [Il. 1. 212]

6-5-6 and I shall send him wherever his heart and spirit urge him. [Od. 16. 81]

6-6-1 idiot? You'll soon pay when the swift hounds devour you [Od. 21. 363]

6-6-2 You would learn what mighty hands I have to back me up. [Od. 20. 237]

6-6-3 In no wise do I think he will take you for himself, nor is it proper. [Od. 21. 322]

6-6-4 here we gather, waiting day after day. [Od. 21. 156]

6-6-5 My child, how long will you go on eating your heart out in sorrow [Il. 24. 128]

6-6-6 Don't dare get it into your mind to escape from me, Dolon. [Il. 10. 447]

Here ends the verses of the Homer oracle.

May it help you!

Short Invocations, prayers, valedictions, maledictions etc

"live long and prosper"
(*Ankh wedja seneb*)
Source: *Contendings of Horus & Seth* (1.6)

"Your shrine is empty"
(*Karya ka shawe*)
Source: *Contendings of Horus & Seth* (3.9_

Offering formula (Osiris version)
"An offering that the King makes
To you Osiris, Lord of Djedu
Great God,
Lord of Abydos
All good things on which the soul lives,
bread, beer, beef, fowl, alabaster & linen

(*Hotep Di Nesew*
Osir neb djedw
Neter Aa
Neb Abdu
Di-ef peret-herew
ta heneqet, ka, aped, shes, menhet)

Source: numberous inscriptions

Offering formula (Sethian version)

"An offering that a king makes

To Set, Bull of Ombos

Great God

Lord of the sky

And heaven's gate

standing at the prow of the sun boat.

A voice offering,

In bread & beer (and linen)

And all things pure & good

On which the God lives"

(*hotep di nesew,*

Set neb nubt,

Neter Aa,

neb peret

Def peret her

te heneqet,

het nebet

neferet wabit

anehet neter im)

Source: "Egyptian Interest in the Oases in the New Kingdom and Colin A. Hope and a New Stela for Seth from Mut el-Kharab" Olaf E. Kaper" *Ramesside Studies in Honour of K A Kitchen*

Maat mantra

"Never did (I) do any evil thing against the people"

(En zep ire khet , djewer remetet)

Source: Tomb of Redi-nes at Giza (G 5032)

"The snake is in my hand and cannot bite me" [107]

Source: Coffin Text 885 ancient words to ward off evil, quoted in Ritner (1993)

General "negative" invocation form:

Be not unaware of me . . . (eg Oh Seth)

Source: Ramesseum Dramatic Papyri (Sethe 1910)

Invocation of Mut

"For those who call me evil, Mut will call them evil"

(Na I Ire dje ben rehorey, dje mewet ben errew)

Source: Ancient Papyrus[115]

---

115. Richard Jasnow & Mark Smith " 'As for Those Who have Called me Evil, Mut will Call them Evil': Orgiastic Cultic Behaviour and its Critics in Ancient Egypt" *Enchoria: Zeitschrift für Demotistik und Koptologie* Band 32 2010/2011 : 25

Appendice: Seven Charakteres (1st version)

1.

We encounter the first of these characteres within the first few lines of the Greek Magical Papyri. And it recurs many times and must therefore be one of the most common. It resembles several hieroglyphs.

The circle occurs in several other sigils and are obviously important signs in their own right - (N33) a grain of sand, pellet or the like. as in grain of gold, medicine or incence. Also (D12) the pupil of the eye - meaning a quarter, a part of the "hekat" measure of corn.

It occurs in many Egyptian spells and even finds its way in the medieval grimoires such as the Key of Solomon, where it is part of the designs on the handle of the magical knife - and this again turns up in the the Gardnerian Book of Shadows. The point is that this is one of the "new" hieroglyphs, that have no fixed meaning, or not one that we understand. Perhaps it was always expressionist, coming straight from the unconscious. Spell PGM I 262-347 says that to invoke the sun God Apollo "take a seven-leafed sprig of laurel and hold it in your right hand / as you summon the heavenly Gods and chthonic daimons. Write on the sprig of laurel the seven characters for deliverance."

As if to illustrate how mutable these techniques might be - the illustration actually has eight characters. So are these seven or eight characters especially connected with deliverance?

2.

The second does actually resemble an Egyptian hieroglyph (D28 in our standard list of signs). It represents two arms, stretching upward, and represents the sound "Ka" meaning "soul" or "spirit":

3.

The third closely resembles the "A" symbol found in any number of languages but not Egyptian. Egyptian being a semitic language "begins" with the "aleph" sound - represented by the Egyptian vulture (G1 in sign list) . I suppose you might just see some similarity between the vulture on its perch and the following sign. It also resembles several signs for man and his occupations - perhaps (A20) which is a man leaning on his staff, the sounds "wr" meaning "elder" or "chief".

4.

The fourth could be one of several Egyptian hieroglyphs especially (T18) & (T19). It could represent a staff, with a blade attached and would then be the word "sms" meaning "bind together". If T19 then the sound would be "ksr" meaning a harpoon, also connected with number 6 below. It also resembles one of the European runes, fehu, uruz or aiwaz:

5.

There are several hieroglyphs that have this box form. Although it could be (Q6) krse - "coffin" which for the Egyptians was an suspicious sign:

6.

The sixth also resembles the Egyptian hieroglyph (N41), the hm sound, meaning a well or cauldron.

7.

Is a much more complex glyph that also resembles several important hieroglyphs, perhaps (R1) "table of offerings", and (R8) the flag, which is an ideogramme for God , sounded as "neter".

8.

And finally this one - which seems to incorporate several heiroglyphs. At first the the whole sigil might look like a doodle. However, if you attempt to copy this you will find that there is more to it than initially meets the eye.

We have a circle: (D12 "pupil of the eye")

Two crossed sticks (Z9 : "to break" - pronounced "swa")

forked stick (U12 : "fork"

Small circles, signifying grains of gold, are a fairly ubiquitous.

Single horizontal line or perhaps circle bisected (N9) by a line, in which case would be "new moon".

So could have also sorts of meanings, perhaps nullifying ("breaking") the malign effects of the new moon.

Index

CPSIA information can be obtained
at www.ICGtesting.com
Printed in the USA
BVHW041409130620
581309BV00006B/144